THE COMPLETE HSA GUIDEBOOK

How to make health savings accounts work for you

TWELFTH EDITION
Includes healthcare reform and tax change updates

Stephen D. Neeleman, M.D.

Copyright © 2018 HealthEquity, Inc. All rights reserved.

No part of this book may be reproduced in any manner whatsoever without written permission except in the case of brief quotations embodied in critical articles and reviews. For information, address HealthEquity, 15 West Scenic Pointe Dr, Ste 100, Draper, UT 84020, 801-727-1000.

ISBN: 978-0-692-95308-2 Printed in the United States of America.

FOREWORD

We began writing the first edition of The Complete HSA Guidebook a few months after the original HSA law became effective on January 1, 2004. It is remarkable to see the change in people's understanding and acceptance of HSAs over the past 14 years. HSAs are becoming a common offering for employers and health plans. Millions of Americans are now using HSAs as an important part of their long-term savings plan.

HealthEquity was founded in 2002 with a simple mission: "We will save healthcare by helping people better save and spend their healthcare dollars." We remain committed to fulfilling our mission of helping people use their HSAs to connect their health and their wealth. As this edition goes to print, HealthEquity members have saved over five billion dollars in their HSAs. National HSA balances are estimated to soon surpass over 50 billion dollars. The money saved in their HSAs cannot only be spent tax-free throughout the course of their lives for their healthcare needs, but at age 65, they can also withdraw their money for non-healthcare needs with the same tax treatment as their 401(k).

During the past 16 years, HealthEquity has grown from a simple idea to one of the largest HSA custodians in the United States. We currently provide HSAs for tens of thousands of employers and millions of consumers. Nearly every day, one of our employers or members asks us if health reform has hurt HSAs. The reality is that provisions within health reform such as guaranteed issue, the "Cadillac Tax," and exchanges have led millions of Americans and their employers to turn to HSA-qualified health plans as the solution to continue to offer valuable insurance and help people avoid taxes today and to save money for the future. Thankfully, HSAs appear to be here to stay, and they will continue to help people better save and spend their healthcare dollars.

Now that the number of Americans with HSAs is reaching critical mass, there are many new companies that offer solutions for wellness, price transparency and telemedicine with the intent to help people make better choices and save money on their healthcare. HealthEquity now partners with many of these companies to offer our members timely, personal, and relevant information and services to help them with their healthcare needs.

Our initial goal with The Complete HSA Guidebook was to create a book about HSAs that was both comprehensive and easy to understand. I believe we accomplished that goal, as many of our readers have commented on the important role The Complete HSA Guidebook has played in helping them better understand HSAs. This edition has been updated to include the most recent regulations from HHS and clarifications from the IRS that affect the HSA law.

I am very appreciative of Sophie Korczyk and Hazel Witte for their work on the first editions. Their legacy is a thoughtful approach to helping our readers understand the complicated tax and insurance laws that affect HSAs. Sadly, Sophie passed away in November 2009.

We remain committed to helping people improve their health and their financial well-being through better understanding and adoption of HSAs. We hope this guidebook remains a powerful tool to accomplish that end.

Stephen D. Neeleman, M.D.
HealthEquity Founder and Vice Chairman
Salt Lake City, Utah
July 2018

This book is intended only as a general explanation of HSAs. It should not be treated as legal reference or in any way considered the provision of legal, financial or tax advice.

HealthEquity, Inc. is a publicly traded (NASDAQ:HQY) non-bank custodian of health savings accounts. Some of the opinions expressed are unique to the way HealthEquity operates and may not be typical. Readers' experience may vary.

In this edition, we have included citations to legal sources. We have cited Internal Revenue Code (26 USC) as of February 2016. We tried to eliminate errors but make no guarantee that the citations are accurate, complete or up-to-date. We shall not be providing corrections or updates to the purchaser or reader. We are not responsible for typographical errors.

As used in this book, "tax-free" refers to federal income tax. HSAs are never taxed at a federal income tax level when used appropriately for qualified medical expenses. Also, most states recognize HSA funds as tax-free with very few exceptions. Please consult a tax advisor regarding your state's specific rules.

The readers should always consult their own legal, tax and financial advisors.

TABLE OF CONTENTS

Chapter 1: How an HSA can benefit you.................1

Chapter 2: HSA-compatible health plans 15

Chapter 3: How to open an HSA......................33

Chapter 4: Contributing to your HSA 41

Chapter 5: Using and growing your HSA.............65

Chapter 6: Becoming a smart healthcare consumer...81

Chapter 7: What if?..................................97

Chapter 8: Using an HSA with other
tax-advantaged accounts 117

Chapter 9: Taxes, paperwork and recordkeeping....125

Chapter 10: Guidelines for employers 143

Chapter 11: Federal and state HSA laws
and healthcare reform...................157

Chapter 12: Connecting health and wealth 165

Appendix..175

Index...211

About the authors 222

CHAPTER 1
How an HSA can benefit you

What is an HSA?

An HSA is a tax-advantaged savings account that belongs to you. It is always paired with a qualified high-deductible health plan (HDHP).

Traditional health plans, like PPOs and HMOs, are typically "use it or lose it". At the end of the year, all of the money you have spent on premiums is gone.

Unlike a traditional health plan, a health savings account (HSA)-qualified high-deductible health plan (HDHP), has a lower premium, and some of the money you would have otherwise spent on premiums can go into your HSA instead. Additionally, you save money on taxes and are given more flexibility and control over your healthcare dollars.

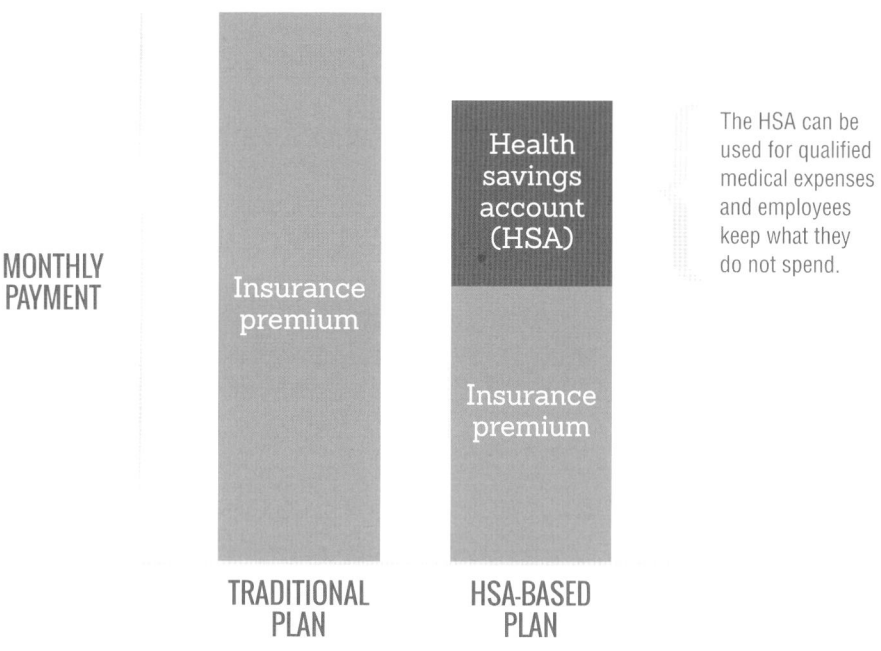

An HSA is administered by a bank, insurance company, or approved third-party custodian or trustee. In most cases, the cash balance is federally-insured. Be sure to read the literature from the custodian or trustee to see whether federal insurance applies to your deposit. Many HSA administrators provide online banking services similar to those of a personal bank account.

You and your employer can make tax-free deposits into your HSA, as long as you are enrolled in a qualified HDHP and you are not also enrolled in other healthcare coverage that will disqualify you. The HDHP protects you from major medical costs, such as catastrophic illness, prolonged hospitalization and excessive medical bills.

The HSA can be used, tax-free, to cover:
- Your insurance deductible
- Qualified healthcare expenses that insurance plans might exclude
- Co-payments and coinsurance until you reach your health plan's out-of-pocket maximum (the HDHP covers the rest)
- Qualified medical, vision or dental expenses that may not be covered by your HDHP.

Know your limits

It is important to know how much you can contribute to your HSA to avoid excess contributions, which are taxed.

2018 and 2019 limits: (Rev. Proc. 2016-28 and 2017-37)

2018	Single	Family
Minimum annual deductible	$1,350	$2,700
Contribution limits	$3,450	$6,900
Out-of-pocket maximum	$6,550	$13,300
2019	Single	Family
Minimum annual deductible	$1,350	$2,700
Contribution limits	$3,500	$7,000
Out-of-pocket maximum	$6,750	$13,500

The money is yours

All of the money in your HSA (including any contributions deposited by your employer) remains yours even if you leave your job, leave your qualifying health plan or retire.

In other words, an HSA is not a "use-it-or-lose-it" type of account (IRC Sec. 223(d)(1)(E)). For this reason, many people use the HSA as an additional savings and investment account for retirement.

You can grow your account through saving and investing

You decide how to use the HSA money, including whether to save it or spend it for healthcare expenses.

As your balance rolls over from year to year, it earns interest. When your balance is large enough, depending on your custodian, you may be able to invest it—tax-free—the same way you can invest dollars from other retirement accounts. Check with your custodian as to whether they offer investment vehicles, and what the minimum requirements are.

You realize free savings

An HSA provides triple-tax savings because:

- Contributions to the HSA are tax-free for you—whether they come from you, your employer, or as gifts from friends or relatives (IRC Sec. 223(a). IRS Notice 2004-2 Q&A 11)

- Unlike a 401(k), the money you and your employer contribute to your HSA through payroll is also not subject to social security (FICA) and Medicare taxes (IRC sec. 106(d)(1), IRS Notice 2004-2 Q&A 19)

- Your account and investment earnings grow tax-free (IRS Notice 2004-2 Q&A 20)

- You can withdraw your money tax-free at any time, as long as you use it for qualified medical expenses (IRC Sec. 223(f)(1))

You have more choice and flexibility in how you pay for healthcare

An HSA-qualified HDHP gives you greater choice and flexibility when managing your healthcare options.

Pay for qualified medical expenses

You can use the HSA to pay for qualified medical expenses for yourself, your spouse and your dependents before the HDHP deductible is met, as well as for other healthcare expenses allowed under Section 213(d) of the Internal Revenue Code (IRC). These are generally the same healthcare expenses individual tax-payers can deduct on their federal income tax returns. The qualified medical expenses are broader than what most health plans cover (IRC Sec. 223(d)(2)(A). IRS Notice 2004-2 Q&A 26. See Appendix C and IRS Publication 502).

Cover work/life transitions

You can use the HSA to bridge events such as unemployment, job changes and periods of disability by paying for health insurance premiums or healthcare directly (IRC Sec. 223(d)(2)(c)(iii), IRS Notice 2004-2 Q&A 27). Your HSA can be used to pay Consolidated Omnibus Budget Reconciliation Act (COBRA) premiums (for continued healthcare coverage through your former employer) (IRC Sec. 223(d)(2)(C)(i), IRS notice 2004-2 Q&A 27), or premiums for long-term care (IRC Sec. 223(d)(2)(C)(ii), IRS Notice 2004-2 Q&A 27).

Cover gaps in care

You can use tax-free HSA dollars for co-payments and deductibles, as well as for services that are not offered by your health plan. You may also pay for services from a physician out of your network with your HSA.

Pay for post-retirement healthcare expenses

HSAs help you save for retirement health expenses tax-free. You can use your HSA to pay for Medicare premiums and out-of-pocket expenses including deductibles, co-pays and coinsurance (except Medigap) (IRC Sec. 223(d)(2)(C)(iv); IRS Notice 2004-2 Q&A 27), including:

- Part A (hospital and inpatient services)
- Part B (physician and outpatient services)
- Part C (Medicare Advantage plans)
- Part D (prescription drugs)

Manage the variability of expenses

The HSA also allows you to deal with the variability of healthcare expenses. For example, one year you may have just a few medical appointments, whereas the next year you may meet your deductible mid-year and still require more appointments.

Because the HSA allows you to reimburse yourself at any time, you can choose to save your money for times when you have more expenses. HSAs can only be used for expenses incurred after the establishment of the HSA (IRS Notice 2004-50 Q&A 39).

By combining HSA funds from the previous year with the funds added during the current year, you may be able to meet all of your costs tax-free.

Benefit from a healthy lifestyle

Effective in 2011, PPACA added PHS Act Sec. 2713. All new HSA-qualified health plans are required to cover 100 percent of standard preventive care services, as designated by your health plan.

If you take advantage of preventive care services and adopt healthy lifestyle habits, your HSA can grow tax-free from year to year and become a significant addition to your retirement nest egg.

Help manage costs

With an HSA-qualified health plan, you have significant power and responsibility over your healthcare decisions. Policymakers hope that by having such a financial incentive, participants become influential healthcare consumers who demand and receive better value with their healthcare spending.

How do HSAs compare to IRAs or 401(k) plans?

HSAs have features in common with retirement accounts, such as individual retirement accounts (IRAs) and 401(k) plans that keep their tax advantages when used for specific purposes. These advantages include year-to-year rollover, portability, choice of account investments and survivor benefits.

Variations on that approach, including Roth IRAs, 529 education accounts and Coverdell accounts, have helped consumers grow their retirement nest eggs using tax-free savings accounts.

How an HSA is like a 401(k) or an IRA

- You and your employer can make pre-tax contributions to your HSA.
- Your contributions roll over from year-to-year.
- Your HSA can grow tax-free for as long as you own the account.
- Your HSA can be inherited by your survivors, but only the spouse can inherit the account as his or her own HSA without being treated as taxable (IRC Sec. 223(f)(B)(A).

How an HSA is better

- You and your employer do not need to pay FICA (Social Security) or Medicare taxes on your HSA contributions made through payroll (IRS Notice 2004-2 Q&A 19).

- You can contribute money from both earned and unearned income up to the IRS yearly limit, as long as you are covered by an HSA-qualified HDHP and are not enrolled in Medicare. Family members and other individuals can contribute to your account; however, only you and your employer may take tax deductions (IRS Notice 2004-2 Q&A 18). Your deduction is limited to the amount of your taxable income. The deduction cannot be carried forward to another year (IRS Notice 2004-2 Q&A 17).

- You can use the money for the qualified medical expenses of your spouse and any of your IRS-qualified dependents—tax-free.

- If you are no longer employed, you can still make contributions to your HSA as long as you are still covered by an HSA-qualified HDHP and are not enrolled in Medicare.

- As long as you use the funds for qualified medical expenses, you are not required to be of retirement age to make tax-free withdrawals at any time without tax or penalty (IRC Sec. 223(f)(1), IRS Notice 2004-2 Q&A 25 & 26).

- After age 65, you can spend the HSA money on non-medical items without paying a 20 percent penalty. However, you will have to pay income tax on distributions if they are not used for qualified medical expenses.

Who can establish and contribute to an HSA?

The IRS has strict guidelines to determine who is eligible to own and contribute to an HSA.

Definition of an eligible individual

Under the law, an eligible individual:

- Must be covered under a qualified HDHP (see chapter 2) on the first day of any month for which eligibility is claimed (IRC Sec. 223(a), IRS notice 2004-2 Q&A 2 through Q&A 7).

- May not be covered under any health plan that is not a qualified HDHP, with the exception of certain permitted coverage and certain health-related payment plans discussed in chapter 2.

- Must not be enrolled in Medicare (the healthcare component of the Social Security program) (IRC Sec. 223(b)(7), IRS Notice 2004-50 Q&A 2 through Q&A 4).

- May not be claimed as a dependent on another individual's tax return (IRC Sec. 223(b)(6)).

Healthcare reform and adult children covered by your HDHP

Under the Patient Protection and Affordable Care Act (PPACA), adult children up to the age of 26 can be covered by their parent's HDHP. This rule for medical coverage should not be confused with whose expenses can be paid from an HSA (see chapter 5). However, if the adult child is self-supporting or does not qualify as a tax deduction, that child cannot use funds from the parent's HSA (IRC Secs. 223(d)(2), 152. Confer: PHS Sec 2714, which added the age 26 rule for medical insured insurance only).

Single adult children who have coverage under a parent's family HDHP can open their own HSAs and contribute up to the yearly family maximum— $6,900 for 2018 or $7,000 for 2019, as long as the adult children are not claimed on another person's tax return (IRC Sec. 223(b)(6), IRS notice 2004-2 Q&A 18). Regardless of the contributions made by the parents into their HSAs, adult children can each contribute the entire family maximum to their own HSAs.

This is an excellent opportunity to set your adult child up with his or her own HSA as a tax-free gift (you do not get to deduct the contribution, but your child can receive it tax-free) (IRS Notice 2004-2 Q&A 18).

Employed individuals

An employer may offer an HDHP with an HSA and pay for some or all of the HDHP premium and contribute an allotted amount toward an HSA. The employer may also offer an HDHP only and allow a certain amount for other benefits, including an HSA, perhaps through a cafeteria plan. In either of these cases, the participant is the eligible individual and owner of the HSA. Therefore, the law's requirements have been met.

Employers may have additional requirements for employees who want to participate in a health plan, including those with an eligible HDHP who want to contribute to an HSA.

These eligibility requirements are separate from those required by law and are part of many employer-sponsored health plans. It is important that employees understand all eligibility requirements in order to reduce misunderstanding or confusion that can occur when a new type of health plan is implemented.

Health plans typically require new employees to work for the employer for a short period of time before becoming eligible to participate. Unless the employee is covered by some other qualifying HDHP during this period, he or she may have to suspend HSA contributions until resuming coverage under a qualified HDHP.

Self-employed individuals

If an individual is a subchapter S owner or self-employed, the individual can open an HSA and make contributions as long as all IRS eligibility requirements are met.

If you are considered a two percent shareholder in an S-corporation, you are not considered an employee. Even if your company sponsors a cafeteria plan under IRC Sec 125, you cannot contribute to the HSA through the cafeteria plan. You can only do so outside of the cafeteria plan (IRC Secs. 125(d)(1)(A), 1372, 318).

Retired and disabled individuals

If an otherwise eligible person is not enrolled in Medicare even though that individual has reached age 65, he or she can contribute to an HSA until the month they are enrolled in Medicare (IRC Sec. 223(b)(7), IRS notice 2004-50 Q&A 2). The individual may also make catch-up contributions prior to their enrollment in Medicare (IRS notice 2004-50 Q&A 3).

You are not eligible to set up an HSA if you do not have an HDHP. Medicare is not an HDHP. If you are enrolled in Medicare, you are ineligible to set up or contribute to an HSA.

Age is not the issue

Regardless of your age, you may still set up and contribute to an HSA as long as you have a qualified HDHP and are not enrolled in Medicare.

If you have an HDHP as well as access to a retirement health reimbursement arrangement (HRA) that provides reimbursement only after you retire, you may still set up an HSA (Rev. Rul. 2004-45 Situation 5).

Disability benefits and HSAs

If you are covered by an HDHP/HSA and qualify for short-term or long-term disability benefits under an employer-sponsored plan, nothing should change if the basic healthcare coverage arrangement remains intact during the disability period.

If you are receiving Social Security Disability benefits, you may cease to be an eligible individual when you become covered by Medicare and cannot continue to contribute to your HSA.

Determining if an HSA is right for you

An HSA allows you to be more involved with decisions on how your healthcare dollars are actually spent and encourages you to budget effectively and save money. In order to think in terms of a healthcare budget, you want to look at your financial situation and the type of healthcare you require.

Consider whether you are eligible to establish and contribute to an HSA, have benefits paid from one, or claim the tax deduction for a contribution. Whether an HDHP/HSA is right for you depends on a number of factors, including the health needs of you and your family, in addition to the frequency you may expect to change jobs or health plans or both.

Do you want to build a fund for healthcare expenses after retirement?

Even with the passage of PPACA and changes in Medicare, post-retirement healthcare costs are expected to escalate rapidly. Industry analysts warn that many retirees will fall short of the amounts needed to cover the gaps in medical coverage as they age.

Without an HSA, many retirees are now paying for the non-covered portion of their medical expenses by taking distributions from their 401(k)s and other retirement savings plans. Unfortunately, these individuals must pay income tax on those distributions (IRC Sec. 402(a)).

With an HSA, a retiree can save significant amounts of money on taxes by paying for qualified medical expenses with pre-tax dollars.

Do you use substantial amounts of healthcare?

Any time you have a choice of health plans, whether from a selection of plans offered by your employer or as an individual purchaser, consider the patterns in your healthcare use.

A chronic condition is one that lasts a long time or recurs frequently and can be treated but not cured. Some people with chronic conditions may need substantial healthcare on an ongoing basis. An HSA may be beneficial for you or a family member who suffers from a chronic disease such as diabetes, heart dysfunction or asthma. Some HDHP policies pay for medications associated with a chronic condition first dollar (not subject to your deductible) under preventive care coverage.

Not all chronic conditions are exceedingly cost-intensive; however, they may need monitoring. Some require medical appliances that are not typically provided by health plans, but are considered medical expenses for purposes of an HSA. Therefore, the expenditure is payable from an HSA.

Before committing to an HSA plan, you will want to compare the flexibility and tax advantages of HSA distributions with the coverage offered by low-deductible, typically higher premium, traditional health plans to determine which option is right for you.

As premiums, co-pays and coinsurance costs all continue to increase in traditional plans, HSA-qualified plans are uniquely positioned to provide long-term savings.

Do you need healthcare coverage for that unanticipated expense or disaster?

Although you and your family may be in good health, healthcare coverage is necessary in the event that a damaging and unanticipated accident may occur.

Acknowledge whether or not you can set aside money in an HSA on a regular basis to cover your annual bout with the flu or your child's ear infection.

Many people do not reach their deductibles because they do not spend much on healthcare. An HSA-qualified health plan may benefit you because it gives you control over your spending and allows you to save tax-free in an account that you can use if and when your healthcare spending increases.

Are you willing to use your plan's network?

HDHPs typically offer networks of providers who have agreed to give special pricing to participants in plans they have contracts with. These discounts lower the amount you may need to pay out of your HSA.

Are you willing to use doctors in your plan's network to lower your healthcare costs? If you decide to go out-of-network, are you willing to pay for the higher costs, possibly out of your HSA or pocket?

The HSA gives you flexibility to go to an out-of-network doctor. If the money is in your HSA, you can pay for that visit.

The HSA-qualified health plan is based on making good choices, both health-wise and budget-wise.

Do you change jobs often?

Consider your job, industry and occupation, as well as your career stage and plans.

People tend to change jobs more often in some fields than in others and younger people tend to move around more than people who are more established in their careers.

HDHPs can be extended under COBRA like any other plan and you can use your HSA to pay COBRA premiums during a period when you lack other coverage

(IRC Sec. 223(d)(2)(C), IRS Notice 2004-2 Q&A 27).

You can continue to use your HSA for healthcare expenses even if you do not have other coverage. An HSA can be an important safety net in a difficult economy.

CHAPTER 2
HSA-compatible health plan

The qualified high-deductible health plan (HDHP)

Before you open an HSA, the IRS requires that you enroll in a qualified high-deductible health plan (HDHP). The HDHP is the insurance component of HSA-based health coverage.

What are the components of an HDHP?

An HDHP has:

- A lower monthly premium than traditional health plans.
- A higher annual deductible than traditional health plans.
- A maximum limit on the total amount you are required to pay out of your own pocket for in-network deductibles, co-payments and coinsurance (premiums are not included in this maximum limit).

Plans that satisfy certain deductible and out-of-pocket limits are referred to as HSA-qualified HDHPs.

The following table shows the minimum annual in-network deductible that a health plan must have in order to qualify as an HDHP. It also shows the maximum annual deductible and other out-of-pocket expenses for HDHPs for 2019 (Rev. Proc. 2015-30).

Tax year 2019		
	Self-only coverage	Family coverage
Minimum annual deductible	$1,350	$2,700
Maximum annual in-network* deductible & other out-of-pocket expenses**	$6,750	$13,500

* This limit does not apply to deductibles and expenses for out-of-network services if the plan uses a network of providers. Only deductibles and out-of-pocket expenses for services within the network are used to figure whether the limit applies.

** If a plan requires an individual to spend more than this amount on the deductible and other out-of-pocket expenses for in-network covered medical expenses, it is not an HSA-qualified HDHP.

Self-only HDHP coverage

Self-only HDHP coverage is an HDHP that covers only one eligible individual.

Family HDHP coverage

Family HDHP coverage is an HDHP that covers an eligible individual and at least one other individual, even if the additional individual is not HSA eligible (for example, if the other individual has a self-only plan that does not allow them to contribute to an HSA).

Example

Family coverage

Bill and Sue are married and have one daughter. Bill selects coverage from his employer that covers his entire family. Sue has her own self-only policy from her employer that is not HDHP-qualified.

Bill can make a full family contribution to an HSA, provided he has no other disqualifying coverage (IRC Sec. 223(b)(5), IRS Notice 2008-59 Q&A 16).

Employee plus one HDHP

If an eligible individual and his or her dependent child are covered under an employee plus one HDHP offered by the individual's employer, the IRS considers them to have family HDHP coverage (IRS Notice 2004-50 Q&A 12).

Family plans that do not meet the high-deductible rule

Some family plans have deductibles for both the entire family and individual family members. If you meet the individual deductible for one family member under these plans, you are not required to meet the higher annual deductible for the family.

If either the deductible for the entire family or the deductible for an individual family member is less than the minimum annual deductible for family coverage allowed by the IRS, then the plan is not considered an HSA-qualified HDHP.

Example

HDHP with both an individual deductible and a family deductible

Elliott has family health insurance coverage for 2019, with an annual deductible of $3,500 and an individual deductible, sometimes called an embedded deductible, of $1,500 for each family member.

The plan does not qualify as an HSA-qualified HDHP, because the deductible for an individual family member is below the minimum annual deductible of $2,700 for family coverage in 2019 (IRS Notice 2004-2 Q&A 3).

What does an HDHP cover?

The purpose of the HDHP is to cover higher, unexpected healthcare expenses that would be difficult to pay for out-of-pocket, even with an HSA.

Under PPACA, HDHPs are also required to pay for preventive care services.

Exactly what your plan covers depends on your employer, your insurer and the choices you make from among the plans available to you. For example, some plans may pay for fertility treatments or bariatric (weight loss) surgery, while others may not.

There are variations among HDHPs, so do not assume that your next plan covers the same things as your last. Be sure you understand your new plan's provisions, found in the summary of benefits you receive during enrollment.

Important insurance terms

There are some terms that will be essential to your understanding of various types of HDHPs, as well as your ability to compare their features.

Eligible individual

You qualify as an eligible individual if you meet the IRS eligibility requirements for opening and contributing to an HSA:

- You must be covered under an HSA-qualified HDHP on the first day of the month in which you open an HSA or make a contribution to an HSA (IRC Sec. 223(c)(1)(A)(i)).

- You have no other health coverage, unless permitted under IRS guidelines (see 'Insurance coverage permitted with an HSA' later in this chapter) (IRC Sec. 223(c)(1)(A)(ii)).

- You are not enrolled in Medicare (IRC Sec. 223(b)(7)).

- You cannot be claimed as a dependent on someone else's tax return (IRC Sec. 223(b)(6)).

Although you must be an eligible individual to open or contribute to an HSA, you do not have to be covered under an HDHP to keep the account, earn tax-free interest and investment dividends, or make tax-free distributions for eligible medical expenses. You get to keep, grow and spend all of the money in the account long after you leave your employer or HDHP (IRS Notice 2004-20 Q&A 20).

Deductible

A deductible is the amount of covered expenses that an individual must pay for a given plan year before the insurance company starts paying covered medical claims. Claims for preventive care are usually paid by the insurance company without requiring you to apply your deductible (see the section on 'First-dollar coverage for preventive care' later in this chapter).

The plan year may be the calendar year (January 1 to December 31), or some other 12-month period that your employer or insurer chooses for managing your plan and keeping track of deductibles and other limits (some plans allow deductibles to accumulate for more than 12 months—see 'Carry-over deductibles' in this section).

To qualify for an HSA in 2019, a single person must have an HDHP with a deductible of at least $1,350. The minimum allowable deductible for a family in 2019 is $2,700 (Rev. Proc. 2016-30).

The HDHP must also have a limit on the maximum deductible and maximum out-of-pocket amounts (it is possible for an HDHP to have a deductible that is too high to qualify for use with an HSA).

The deductible and out-of-pocket limits are subject to change annually due to increases in the consumer price index (CPI). The IRS typically announces changes to these limits in May or June, the year before they change.

Tax year 2019		
	Self-only coverage	Family coverage
Minimum annual deductible	$1,350	$2,700
Maximum annual in-network* deductible and other out-of-pocket expenses**	$6,750	$13,500

* This limit does not apply to deductibles and expenses for out-of-network services if the plan uses a network of providers. Instead, only deductibles and out-of-pocket expenses for services within the network should be used to figure whether the limit applies (IRS Notice 2004-2 Q&A 4).

** If a plan requires an individual to spend more than this amount on the deductible and other out-of-pocket expenses for covered medical expenses, it is not an HSA-qualified HDHP.

Not all HDHPs meet IRS requirements. A plan with a deductible that is too high will be disqualified for use with an HSA.

Embedded deductibles (IRS Notice 2004-50 Q&A 20)

Some HDHPs provide multiple deductibles or embedded deductibles. In such plans, the lowest deductible is the one that determines whether the plan is a qualified HDHP.

Example

Family plan with embedded deductibles that disqualify the plan as an HDHP

The Jones family is covered under a plan that provides family coverage with a per-person embedded deductible of $1,000 and a total family deductible of $2,700 (also called an umbrella deductible).

The plan begins paying for care for individuals in the family who exceed $1,000 in expenses, regardless of whether the total $2,700 family deductible has been met.

Mr. Jones incurs covered medical expenses of $1,500 during the year.

The plan pays benefits of $500 on his behalf, even though the $2,700 family deductible has not been met.

Since claims are paid by the insurance company for individuals before they reach the $2,700 minimum HDHP family deductible for the plan year, the plan is not a qualified HDHP, and the family therefore is not eligible to contribute to an HSA.

Without the $1,000 per-person deductible, however, the plan would be an eligible HDHP (IRS Notice 2004-50 Q&A 20).

Carry-over deductible (IRS Notice 2004-50 Q&A 24)

Some insurance carriers allow expenses that were applied to the previous deductible to be applied, or carried over, to the new policy when the plan year resets. Usually, the carry-over deductible is applied for expenses incurred at the end of the plan year during a certain period of time (usually one to three months before the plan year's end).

This is not a requirement, but it is an added benefit when expenses occur late in the year. In some circumstances this type of carry-over deductible will exclude your plan from being HSA-qualified. Because the deductible includes more than 12 months, the IRS minimum deductible limit (based on a 12-month plan year) must be increased.

Example

Carry-over deductible

Matt has a plan that allows him to include expenses from 15 months (three month carry-over) to satisfy the deductible.

To be an HSA-qualified HDHP, an individual policy must have a minimum deductible in 2019 of $1,688 (15/12 x $1,350 = $1,688). A family policy must have a minimum deductible of $3,375 (15/12 x $2,700 = $3,375).

If Matt's plan does not satisfy these increased minimums, it is not considered a qualified HDHP.

First-dollar coverage for preventive care

First-dollar coverage is payment for care prior to requiring you to meet your deductible.

Beginning September 23, 2010, PPACA required all new group health plans and plans in the individual market to provide first-dollar coverage for preventive services rated A or B by the U.S. Preventive Services Task Force. These include recommended immunizations, preventive care for infants, children, and adolescents, as well as additional preventive care and screenings for women.

HSA-qualified HDHPs generally comply with PPACA requirements. Check with your health plan or benefits team to determine which specific preventive care services are covered.

Preventive care includes, but is not limited to the following: (See IRS Notice 2004-23)

- Periodic health evaluations, including tests and diagnostic procedures ordered in connection with routine examinations, such as annual physicals
- Routine prenatal and well-child care
- Child and adult immunizations
- Tobacco cessation programs
- Obesity weight-loss programs
- Screening services, including screening services for the following:
  - Cancer
  - Heart and vascular diseases
  - Infectious diseases
  - Mental health conditions
  - Substance abuse
  - Metabolic, nutritional and endocrine conditions
  - Musculoskeletal disorders
  - Obstetric and gynecological conditions
  - Pediatric conditions
  - Vision and hearing disorders

Important details

- If your health plan uses a network of providers, be aware that health plans are only required to provide these preventive services through an in-network provider. Your health plan may allow you to receive these services from an out-of-network provider, but they may charge you additional fees.
- To know which covered preventive services are right for you—based on your age, gender and health status—ask your healthcare provider.

IRS rules for preventive care benefits

Even with the passage of healthcare reform, IRS rules for first-dollar coverage remain in place. The IRS states that benefits eligible for first-dollar coverage can include:

(IRC Sec. 223(c)(2)(C), IRS Notice 2004-50 Q&As 26 and 27, IRS Notice 2004-23, IRS Notice 2013-57).

- Periodic health evaluations, including tests and diagnostic procedures ordered in connection with routine examinations, such as annual physicals
- Routine prenatal and well-child care
- Child and adult immunizations
- Tobacco cessation programs
- Obesity weight-loss programs
- Screening services
- Some medications which are intended to prevent disease (such as high blood pressure or high cholesterol medications)

The definition of preventive care that applies to HSA-qualified HDHPs generally excludes any service or benefit intended to treat an existing illness, injury or condition. However, in situations where it would be unreasonable to perform another procedure to treat the condition, incidental or ancillary treatments to a preventive care screening or service are allowed.

If you have questions about whether the new healthcare reform provisions apply to your particular plan, contact your insurer or plan administrator. If you still have questions, contact your state insurance department.

Network plans

A network plan (such as a PPO) is a health plan that generally accommodates favorable pricing and benefits for services provided by its network of providers, as opposed to services provided outside of the network.

Repricing

If your HDHP is a network plan, your expenses will be repriced if you use in-network healthcare providers. Repricing refers to the adjustment of healthcare providers' prices to reflect discounts the providers have negotiated with your health plan.

Network plans and repricing are both allowable, but are not required, in qualified HDHPs.

Separate out-of-pocket limits

Network plans may provide a different level of benefits for members when they use in-network versus out-of-network providers. Many of these plans have separate out-of-pocket limits and deductibles for network and non-network care. This provides a powerful incentive for plan participants to use network providers.

The law does not specify a maximum out-of-pocket limit for spending on non-network care, so an HDHP may have higher out-of-pocket limits for services provided outside the network than the $6,650/$13,300 limits for 2018 and the $6,750/$13,500 limits for 2019.

Usual, customary and reasonable amounts

A plan may also restrict benefits to what is considered usual, customary and reasonable amounts. Any expenses above that amount that are not paid by an HDHP are not required to be included in determining maximum out-of-pocket expenses

(IRS Notice 2004-50 Q&A 16).

Example

Fee charged by an out-of-network provider

Your plan determines that the reasonable cost of a certain type of surgery is $2,000, a price it has negotiated with its in-network providers. You go to an out-of-network provider and the bill totals $2,500. The health plan will pay only $2,000 of this bill, and the additional $500 you have to pay may not apply to your health plan's out-of-pocket limit.

Inquire as to whether your HDHP has separate limits for in- and out-of-network providers and whether its network includes the providers you want to use for medical care. You may obtain this information by speaking with your employer's benefits administrator, your insurance plan, your HR team, or by reading the summary of plan benefits available from your plan or given to you during open enrollment.

Co-payments and coinsurance

A co-payment is a fixed-dollar payment a patient makes per doctor visit, treatment, study or prescription.

Coinsurance is the percentage of an insurance claim for which the patient is responsible.

Out-of-pocket maximum

The out-of-pocket maximum is the highest amount of money you have to pay during a plan year. In some HDHPs, the out-of-pocket maximum and the deductible are the same amount.

However, many plans do not completely cover expenses once you have reached the deductible. In the following scenario, a plan may "split the bill" with a member until the out-of pocket maximum is reached. This is called coinsurance.

Example

Out-of-pocket maximum

Tricia has a deductible of $1,500 and an out-of-pocket maximum of $3,000.

Tricia pays up to her $1,500 deductible, after which her plan agrees to split the bill 80/20. The plan will pay 80 percent of covered medical expenses after the deductible, and Tricia will pay 20 percent in coinsurance.

If Tricia has additional expenses after she reaches her deductible, she will pay 20 percent of those bills until she spends another $1,500 in out-of-pocket expenses.

At this point, her total spending will have reached $3,000. She has hit her out-of-pocket maximum, and her insurance plan will pay 100 percent of the rest of her covered medical expenses for that plan year.

With HDHPs, the amounts you pay for deductibles, co-payments or coinsurance are included in your out-of-pocket expenses, which are kept as a running total.

Insurance premiums you pay are not included toward out-of-pocket limits
(IRS Notice 2004-50 Q&A 21).

Once you have reached your plan's limit for the year, remaining in-network eligible expenses are covered 100 percent, regardless of the plan's usual co-payment or coinsurance arrangements. Some plans refer to this limit as the stop-loss limit.

In 2019, a qualified HDHP's out-of-pocket limits must be no higher than $6,750 per year for individual coverage and no higher than $13,500 per year for family coverage; though they can be lower.

If a plan has multiple out-of-pocket maximums, the sum of these limits must be equal to, or less than the amount required by law.

Remember, the maximum out-of-pocket expenses allowed by law are for in-network care only. Health plans will most likely require higher out-of-pocket expenses for out-of-network care.

Example (See IRS Notice 2004-50 Q&A 20, Example 1)

Multiple out-of-pocket maximum limits for a family

Dean, Laurie and their two children have a family plan. Their plan specifies that each family member's in-network, out-of-pocket maximum is $3,000, after which the plan pays 100 percent for each member who reaches that maximum.

Since the 2019 HDHP out-of-pocket maximum per family member by law is $13,500, their plan would be a qualified HDHP (4 x $3,000 = $12,000).

However, if they had four children, their plan would not be a qualified HDHP, because the maximum out-of-pocket limit would be higher than the legal maximum (6 x $3,000 = $18,000).

Yearly and lifetime limits

Before healthcare reform, if you exceeded your plan's yearly or lifetime benefit limits for a medical condition, you had to use your HSA or other funds to make up the difference.

PPACA now prohibits insurers from imposing lifetime limits on benefits. This provision became effective September 23, 2010, and affects all existing insurance plans.

If you have been using your HSA or other funds to pay for treatments that exceeded your plan's annual limits, you may be able to stop and have the plan pick up the cost again. Contact your insurance company to find out when it will put this option into effect.

Insurance coverage permitted with an HSA

The IRS is very strict about what kinds of insurance you can have along with an HSA-qualified HDHP. Having another policy with benefits that overlap some of the medical coverage in your HDHP can make you ineligible to contribute to an HSA.

The listed benefits outlined below are among some of the insurance policies that can result in ineligibility.

Prescription drug benefits

Some plans offer prescription drug benefits through separate plans (also called pharmacy riders) that cover prescription drugs outside of any deductibles that apply to other services covered under the plan. Such prescription drug benefits are not considered permitted coverage under HSA law, unless these riders are specifically designed for preventive care medications (IRS Notice 2004-50 Q&A 26).

A participant covered by an HDHP that meets the law's requirements and is also covered by a non-preventive prescription drug plan or rider that provides benefits before the HDHP's deductible is met may not open or contribute to an HSA. This is because the prescription plan provides first-dollar coverage for a benefit that is not permitted.

Discount cards

Discount cards that entitle you to price reductions on services or health products, such as prescription drugs, are allowed with the HSA as long as you are required to pay the cost of the items (at the reduced rate), until your deductible is met (IRS Notice 2004-50 Q&A 9).

Hospitalization indemnity plans

In order to qualify for benefits under hospitalization indemnity plans, you must be admitted to a hospital.

An indemnity plan is one that pays health insurance benefits in the form of cash payments rather than services, typically as a fixed cash amount each day you are in the hospital. Some insurance companies may call these plans gap plans or HSA protector policies, because one function of such plans is to cover you against a large bill before you meet your HDHP's deductible.

This can serve to protect your HSA dollars, or to help pay for hospital expenses before you have had time to build your account balance.

HSA-qualified indemnity or gap plans cannot cover outpatient hospital services, such as medical tests you might have in a hospital or hospital-related facility without being admitted to the hospital. In other words, the indemnity plan is not intended to cover relatively small expenses just because they are incurred in the hospital rather than in a freestanding facility.

Care from IHS or the VA

Individuals who receive care from IHS (Indian Health Service) or the VA (Veteran Administration) are subject to the three month rule, if the services provided are not dental, vision or preventive care (IRS Notice 2012-14 (OJS) and IRS Notive 20004-50 Q&A 5 (VA)). An individual is not eligible to make HSA contributions for any month in which they have received medical benefits from the VA or an IHS facility at any time during the previous three months. However, if their spouse meets the eligibility requirements, then the spouse may contribute the full family maximum and pay for the family's expenses from their health savings account. Veterans are not subject to the three-month rule when receiving treatment for a service-connected disability (IRC Sec. 223(c)(1)(C) Section 4007(b) of the Surface Transportation Act of 2015 (HR 3236) IRS Notice 2015-87 Q&A 20).

Other permitted and non-permitted coverage

(See IRC Sec. 223(c)(1)(B) and (c)(3), IRS Notice 2004-50 Q&A 7 through 10).

The tax code and the IRS have specific rules for insurance plans that are allowed to coexist with an HSA and plans that would disqualify you from owning an HSA. For a quick summary, see the following tables:

Allowed

- Automobile, dental, vision and long-term care insurance
- Coverage for a specific disease or illness as long as it pays a specific dollar amount when the policy is triggered; or indemnity plans that pay a fixed amount per day or other period of hospitalization
- Wellness programs offered by employers, if they do not pay significant medical benefits
- FSAs or HRAs that are limited purpose (limited to dental, vision, or preventive care) or post-deductible (pay for medical expenses after the plan deductible is met) (Rev. Rul. 2004-45)
- An employer-sponsored HRA that can only be used when you retire or after you meet your annual deductible
- A high-deductible, non-HDHP (PPO, HMO), if the deductible meets or exceeds the HDHP required minimum
- An embedded individual deductible in your family HDHP coverage, if it is not less than the minimum required family HDHP deductible (IRS Notice 2004-50 Q&A 20)
- Worker's compensation insurance
- Tort liability payments
- Prescription or other discount programs that are not insurance

Not allowed

- Spouse's flexible spending account (FSA) or health reimbursement arrangement (HRA), if it can pay for any kind of qualified medical expense before the HDHP deductible is met (See Rev. Rul. 2004-45)
- Employer payments or reimbursements for medical expenses below the minimum HDHP deductible
- General FSAs or HRAs that pay for any kind of qualified medical expense before the HDHP deductible is met
- Medicare (IRC Sec. 223(b)(7))
- Health benefits or prescription drugs received from the Veterans Administration or one of its facilities in the last three months. However, beginning 1/1/2016, hospital care or medical services received under any law administered by the Secretary of Veterans Affairs for a service-connected disability is considered allowable coverage (Section 223(c)(1)(C) as amended to Surface Transportation Act (HR 3236)) (IRS Notice 2004-50 Q&A 5)
- TRICARE (IRS Notice 2004-50 Q&A 6)

CHAPTER 3
How to open an HSA

To open an HSA, you must be enrolled in a qualified HDHP and be otherwise eligible as of the first day of the month you want to open your account.

See chapter 2 for a description of an HSA-qualified HDHP. Your insurance provider, broker or employer can also help you find the right plan.

Find the right HSA provider

HSAs must be held by a financial institution

You cannot simply set aside your HSA contributions in a shoebox, safe-deposit box or ordinary bank or other account—the money has to be set aside in an account specifically designated as an HSA.

What a custodian does

The HSA trustee or custodian holds your balances, receives and records contributions, and processes distributions. The custodian also prepares the appropriate tax forms for you at the end of the year.

In general, an insurance company or a bank can be an HSA trustee or custodian, as can any entity approved by the Internal Revenue Service (IRS) as a trustee or custodian for individual retirement accounts (IRAs).

Other entities may request approval to be an HSA trustee or custodian under IRS regulations.

Not all of these companies provide the same level of service or support. Do your homework about the quality of product and service offered before you sign up with an HSA custodian.

Choosing an HSA custodian

You may be setting up an HSA on your own, or your employer may make arrangements for you to establish an HSA with a particular HSA administrator.

Your HDHP and HSA do not have to be managed by the same company; you may prefer the service, terms and investment opportunities of an HSA provider independent from your insurance company.

It is important that your expectations for the basic administration of your HSA are clear. Some of the issues you should review include fees, investment earnings and how your account will be managed.

Get answers to the following questions, so your HSA runs smoothly

- How much should I contribute and how often?
- Can I make a contribution monthly, quarterly or with any payroll?
- What methods can I use to make contributions?
- How often do I receive a statement?
- How often can I increase or decrease my contributions?
- When will I receive my debit card and other welcome materials?
- What should I do if I need to use the account before I receive my debit card?

Ask the following questions about fees

- **How are fees set?** It costs money to manage your account, keep records and send out the appropriate forms and statements.

- **Is the fee based on the amount in my account or on how much I contribute monthly? Or is it a fixed fee that is independent of how much I have in my HSA? Are fees waived if my balance reaches a certain level?**

- **Which fees can be assessed?** Some possible fees include those for account maintenance, replacement of lost or stolen checks, stop-payment charges if you should have a dispute with a healthcare provider, or if an erroneous charge to your account is made.

- **Will I be charged a fee if the account is rolled over to another custodian or permanently closed?** The disclosure rules apply to account fees and depend on the custodian selected. Fee disclosure rules are different for banks, insurance companies, mutual funds and other entities.

- **If my account is offered through my employer, who pays the fees? Me or my employer? Can I pay fees directly or do they have to be paid from my account? Do fees count against the amount I can spend?**

Ask the following questions about account earnings

- **What is the rate of return on my account?** For instance, what interest rate does it earn, and how is it compounded?

- **What is the minimum balance threshold in order to make investments?**

- **Is there a charge to make investments or is there a minimum amount of money that must be invested?**

- **Are investment earnings on my account ever forfeitable? Does the account carry investment risk? Is it federally-insured?** HSA custodians can offer account holders an federally-insured account, which earns a modest interest rate while the principal is guaranteed by the FDIC up to the balance limit. Most HSA custodians also offer a platform of self-directed mutual funds. These funds are usually publicly traded offering investment in stocks and bonds. The principal balance of mutual funds is not guaranteed. It is subject to market risk and will fluctuate in value resulting in potential losses and gains over time. Investors should carefully consider information contained in the fund prospectus including investment objectives, risks, charges and expenses.

Some account management issues to understand

- **Can my creditors seize balances in my HSA in the event I declare personal bankruptcy?** For more information about HSAs and bankruptcy, see chapter 7—'What if?.'

- **Does the account trustee or custodian impose limits on the size or number of distributions that I can take during a given period?**

- **Does the account trustee or custodian accept rollovers or trustee-to-trustee transfers from other eligible accounts?** Trustees and custodians may accept rollovers and transfers, but they are not required to.

- **How easy is it to move money from an investment account back to the HSA if needed for a large medical expense? Is there a waiting period? Are there extra fees?**

- **Does the custodian or trustee provide a broad range of investments that suit your needs?**

Ask about additional services

Healthcare cost structures can be confusing. Prices are not always readily apparent. As an HSA owner, you should maximize your investment and spend your money wisely.

Some forward-thinking HSA providers offer services to assist you in making smart choices. Make sure to find out if your potential HSA provider offers value-added services to help you better save and spend your healthcare dollars.

- Will I have access to quality cost comparison tools from my employer, health plan or HSA custodian?
- Does the account trustee or custodian provide phone and/or online help to assist me in reviewing and minimizing my healthcare spending?
- When is phone support available? What if I have an emergency in the middle of the night?
- What types of services are provided with a mobile application for my smart phone or tablet?
- What is the easiest way for me to save my receipts for future healthcare spending?
- Does my custodian provide simple-to-use investment options and advice to help me grow my HSA balance?
- Does my custodian charge me to invest my HSA dollars?

Opening the account

You can open your HSA any time throughout the year, as long as you are already enrolled in a qualified HDHP. Most people enroll in their HSA during their employer's yearly benefits open enrollment period.

Where to enroll

In most cases, you will go to your employee benefits or HR website to enroll online.

If you are opening your account independent of your employer, then the HSA provider you select should have an easy-to-use online enrollment process.

If you are opening an HSA at a regular bank, then you can enroll in person or on the bank's website.

Your insurance broker or health plan should also have forms or websites to help you enroll in an HSA.

Signing a custodial agreement

Your HSA provider will require you to sign a custodial agreement or a trust agreement, or otherwise enroll as part of your employer-based health insurance program.

Some HSA administrators do not require "wet signatures" or paper forms if the enrollment process is tied to enrolling for the HDHP. In that case, you can enroll online at the same time you enroll in your insurance plan.

To see what a trust or a custodial agreement looks like, see IRS Form 5305-B and 5305-C.

Customer Identification Program (CIP)

As part of the USA Patriot Act, when an HSA is opened, the account holder goes through a verification process. All financial institutions are required to verify the name, date of birth, social security number and address of each account holder. The USA Patriot Act verification process applies to all financial accounts (HR 3162, Public Law 107-56).

Designating a beneficiary

Once your HSA is set up, you should designate a beneficiary. If your beneficiary is your spouse, then he or she will become the owner of the HSA if you die. The HSA will be included in your estate for other named beneficiaries. See chapter 7 under 'What if I die?' for more information.

Receiving your welcome kit, debit card, or checkbook

Once your HSA is open, you may receive a debit card and/or checkbook from your HSA administrator. Doctor visits will remain the same, except you may be required to pay at the time of service.

If your HDHP is a network plan and you use its providers, then your bill may be sent to your insurance company first for repricing, and will be returned to you for payment at a discounted rate.

Ask your healthcare provider to contact your health plan for claim submission information. Your HSA administrator and your health plan can assist you if you have questions.

CHAPTER 4
Contributing to your HSA

Who can contribute to your HSA?

Anyone (employer, family member, or any other person) may contribute to an HSA on behalf of an eligible HSA holder.

Even state governments are able to make HSA contributions on behalf of eligible individuals who are insured under health plans or state high-risk pools that qualify as HDHPs (IRS Notice 2004-50 Q&A 29).

Who gets the tax breaks?

HSA contributions are tax-deductible, grow tax-free and are never taxed if used for qualified medical expenses. However, only you and your employer can claim a tax deduction when a contribution to your account is made.

Others who contribute to your account are unable to take a tax deduction. However, it is not required that their contributions toward your HSA count toward your gross income. In other words, all contributions to your HSA, no matter the source, are tax-free to you (IRS Notice 2004-2 Q&A 18 and 19).

HSAs are funded on a pre-tax basis. For an individual, it is an above-the-line deduction, independent of whether or not you itemize (IRS Notice 2004-2 Q&A 17).

Employer contributions are not taxable to the employee, nor are they subject to employment taxes, such as Social Security payroll taxes or the federal portion of taxes that finance unemployment benefits (IRS Notice 2004-2 Q&A 19). The earned income credit (EIC) is not affected by employer contributions (IRS Notice 2004-50 Q&A 85).

Self-employed individuals and 2 percent owners of S corporations are not considered employees. As such, they cannot receive employer contributions. However, they can make contributions on their own, and claim the above-the-line deduction on their personal income taxes.

Contributions made by an individual are taken as a deduction on Federal Form 1040, and you are therefore not required to itemize in order to receive the tax break. Your employer will report the employer HSA contributions on your Form W-2. Your HSA trustee or custodian will report distributions to you and the IRS on Form 1099-SA and contributions on Form 5498-SA.

Note: There is no place to take the deduction on Federal Forms 1040A and 1040EZ.

Who owns the HSA and the contributions?

(IRC Sec. 223(d)(1)(E)) (IRS Notice 2004-50 Q&A 81)

HSA dollars are owned by you, the account holder, and they cannot be taken by the employer's creditors in the event of a company lawsuit or company bankruptcy.

Unused money rolls over to the next year and is fully portable. This means you take it with you in the event that you leave your employer, your employer changes health plans, or you change your health plan.

An account beneficiary's interest in an HSA is not forfeitable, so an employer cannot recoup any contribution previously made to your HSA.

Example

Employee quits before completing a full year of employment

Ken's employer contributed $2,000 to his HSA on January 1 expecting that he would work through December 31.

Ken terminated his employment on May 3.

His employer may not recoup any portion of its contribution to Ken's HSA.

Yearly contribution limits

The maximum amount you can contribute to your HSA is determined by the IRS. All HSA holders with a qualified plan may contribute up to these limits.

The limit for individuals in 2018 is $3,450 and for families is $6,900. The limit for individuals in 2019 is $3,500 and for families is $7,000. Individuals age 55 and older can make an additional annual catch-up contribution of $1,000.

The following table shows the maximum allowed contribution limits for a total contribution (from all sources) over a year, though HSA holders and employers can contribute less if desired:

HSA contribution limit	2018	2019
Individual	$3,450	$3,500
Family	$6,900	$7,000
Additional catch-up contribution for those 55+	$1,000	$1,000

The same annual contribution limit applies regardless of who contributes. These contribution limits are set by law, and they are updated each year to allow for inflation.

Example

An employer contributes to an employee's HSA

Jerome and Taneesha are married and have a qualified HDHP with a family deductible of $3,500 effective January 1, 2019.

Jerome's employer contributes $85 per month to his HSA, for a total of $1,020 per year.

Jerome's maximum 2019 HSA contribution limit is $7,000, so he can personally contribute up to an additional $5,980.

He can also choose to deposit less, or nothing, into his account.

Catch-up contributions for individuals 55 years of age and older (IRC Sec. 223(b)(3))

For individuals 55 and older, catch-up contributions can be made to their HSA.

Similar to an IRA, the money remaining in HSAs rolls over from year-to-year. Like IRA owners, HSA owners age 55 and older can contribute more, in hopes of boosting the savings in their HSA. These catch-up amounts are as follows:

- 2018: $1,000
- 2019: $1,000

Catch-up contributions for spouses (IRS Notice 2004-2 Q&A 14)

If each spouse is 55 or older, then both spouses must have individual HSAs for each to make a catch-up contribution. A married couple with two HSAs may make catch-up contributions totaling $2,000 in 2018 and 2019.

All contributions must cease once an individual enrolls in Medicare, as they are no longer in an HSA-qualified health plan. However, they can continue to invest the money and take distributions for qualified medical expenses.

Contributing to your HSA | 45

Example

Married couple making catch-up contributions

If Roger and Noelle are both older than 55 and neither is covered by Medicare, then they can contribute an additional $2,000 ($1,000 each) to their individual HSAs for 2018 and 2019.

If only Roger has an HSA, he can contribute an extra $1,000 as a catch-up contribution.

More options at age 65 and after

If you choose to enroll in Medicare at the age of 65 or older, you may still use your HSA for healthcare expenses. However, you will not be allowed to make further contributions, as you are no longer enrolled in a qualified HDHP.

If you decide to delay your enrollment in Medicare, you can continue to make contributions past the age of 65, as long as you are still covered by an HSA-qualified HDHP. In addition, you can also continue to make $1,000 yearly catch-up contributions (IRS Notice 2004-50 Q&A 2).

Opening an HSA mid-year

New account holders who enroll in an HDHP and open an HSA mid-year have two choices:

- Contribute a prorated amount for the actual number of months they are eligible during the year.

- Take advantage of the IRS full-contribution rule and contribute the entire yearly maximum for their age and level of coverage.

Prorating the maximum yearly contribution

If you are not certain that you will still be enrolled in your HDHP during the entire next tax year, then you can contribute a prorated amount for the months you are actually eligible in the current tax year.

To do this, divide the yearly allowable maximum contribution by 12, then multiply the result by the number of months you are eligible during that tax year.

Example

Contributing a prorated amount for a partial year of eligibility

Carlos started a new job in September and enrolled as an individual (single-only) in his company's qualified HDHP on October 1, 2019.

He was told that his assignment would not be considered permanent until the end of his company's standard six-month probationary period.

Carlos wants to contribute as much as possible to his HSA, but there are only three months left in the year and he has no guarantee that he will be employed and covered by his HDHP the entire following year.

Carlos decides to prorate his contribution for the months he is actually enrolled in the HDHP in the current year.

He divides his yearly maximum contribution by 12 (1/12 of $3,500 = $291.67).

The prorated amount that Carlos can contribute for the current year is 3 months x $291.67, or $875.01.

Full-contribution or last-month rule

The full-contribution rule (also known as the last-month rule) allows individuals who are eligible on the first day of the last month of their tax-paying year (December 1 for most tax-payers) to be considered eligible for the entire year. Therefore, under these circumstances, you can contribute up to the full yearly maximum for your coverage type (self or family).

In this case, an eligible individual is considered enrolled in the same HDHP coverage (i.e., self-only or family coverage) as he or she has previously been on the first day of the last month of the year. For example, if an individual first becomes HSA-eligible on December 1, 2018, and has family HDHP coverage, then he or she is considered an eligible individual having family HDHP coverage for all 12 months of 2018.

The full contribution rule also applies to catch-up contributions made by eligible individuals age 55 and older who are allowed to contribute an additional $1,000 each year.

The full-contribution rule applies regardless of whether the individual was eligible for the entire year, had HDHP coverage for the entire year or had disqualifying non-HDHP coverage for part of the year. However, a testing period applies for purposes of the full-contribution rule. If you fail to maintain an HSA-qualified HDHP during the entire testing period, you will have to pay taxes and penalties for making an excess contribution.

- If you have single-only HDHP coverage, you can contribute the entire $3,450 for 2018. If you are 55 years of age or older, you can also contribute the entire catch-up contribution of $1,000, for a total of $4,450 for 2018.

- If you have family HDHP coverage, you can contribute the entire $6,900 for 2018 (plus the annual catch-up contribution if you are 55 or older).

Example

Using the full-contribution rule to make the largest allowable HSA contribution

Roberto's HDHP coverage started on November 10, 2018. Because he has HDHP coverage by December 1, he can contribute $3,450 to his HSA as if he had been in the HDHP the entire year.

Karl joined his HDHP on November 30, 2018. He waits until February 2019 to open his HSA. The IRS allows account holders to make 2018 contributions until April 15, 2019, so Karl makes a lump sum contribution of $3,450 for 2018. He also starts contributing for 2019 by setting up regular payroll deductions.

Nancy joined her HDHP on December 2, 2018. She cannot make a full-year contribution for 2018 like Roberto and Karl did because she missed the December 1 deadline for being in a qualified HDHP. In fact, she cannot contribute for the month of December, because she has to be in an HDHP on the first day of the month in which she makes a contribution to her HSA. The first day she is eligible to contribute to her HSA is January 1, 2019.

Testing period

Under the full-contribution rule, the testing period begins with the last month of your tax year and ends on the last day of the twelfth month following that month. For example, December 1, 2018, through December 31, 2019.

If contributions were made to your HSA based on your eligibility for the entire year under the full-contribution rule, then you must remain an eligible individual during the entire testing period. If you fail to remain an eligible individual during the testing period (with the exception of death or disability), you must include the total number of contributions made to your HSA that would not have otherwise been made, apart from the full-contribution rule, as income.

This amount must be included in your income in the year that you fail to be an eligible individual. This amount is also subject to an additional 10 percent tax. Income and additional tax are shown on IRS Form 8889, Part III.

Example

Not remaining an eligible individual for the entire testing period

Chris, age 53, becomes an eligible individual on December 1, 2018. He has family HDHP coverage on that date. Under the last-month rule, he can contribute $6,900 into his HSA for 2018.

Chris stops being an eligible individual in June 2019 when he drops his HDHP coverage. Because Chris did not remain an eligible individual during the testing period (December 1, 2018, through December 31, 2019), the contributions made in 2017 that would not have been made without the full-contribution rule must be included in his 2018 income.

Chris uses the worksheet for line 3 of IRS Form 8889 instructions to determine this amount.

January	0
February	0
March	0
April	0
May	0
June	0
July	0
August	0
September	0
October	0
November	0
December	$6,900
Total for all months	$6,900

Divide total by 12 for monthly contribution $575.00.

Chris would include $6,325.00 ($6,900 minus the $575.00 that was allowable for the one month he was eligible in 2017) in his gross income on his 2018 tax return. Also, an additional 10 percent tax applies to the $6,325.00 he over-contributed in 2018.

Contributing to your HSA | 51

Example

Making a maximum contribution late in the calendar year—then leaving the HDHP early

Sixty-year-old Lian started a new job. She enrolled in her HDHP and HSA on June 1, 2018.

Because she planned to retire in five years, she wanted to build all of her retirement accounts as quickly as possible. She decided to take advantage of the full-contribution rule and contribute the maximum yearly amount in her HSA ($3,450 plus her catch-up contribution of $1,000 = $4,450).

Because she started her new job on June 1, Lian was in a qualified HDHP for only seven months in 2018.

Lian knew she would need to remain in a qualified HDHP until December 31, 2019 to avoid taxes and penalties on the extra amount she contributed in 2018.

Unfortunately, Lian's employer laid her off in March 2019.

Lian realized that because she did not stay in her employer's HDHP during the entire testing period (December 1, 2018 through December 31, 2019), she would have to pay income tax and 10 percent additional tax on the amount she over-contributed for 2018.

To see what she would have to pay, she divided the amount she contributed in 2018 by 12 to get the prorated monthly amount.

$4,450/12 = $370.83

Then, she multiplied the monthly prorated amount by five to get the amount she overcontributed for the five months when she was not enrolled in an HDHP in 2018.

5 x $370.83 = $1,854.15

She prepared to add the $1,854.15 to her adjusted gross income on her 2018 tax return and pay an additional 10 percent tax ($185.41).

Example (continued)

The better ending

Wisely, Lian talked to a tax adviser as soon as she was laid off. The tax adviser told her that continuing her HDHP coverage under COBRA until December 31, 2019 would satisfy the testing period.

The tax adviser gave Lian more good news. The law allowed Lian to use her HSA funds to pay the COBRA premiums (IRC Sec. 223(d)(2)(C)(i), IRS Notice 2004-2 Q&A 27).

Not only did she avoid the tax and penalty, she also had continued health insurance coverage throughout the rest of 2019, even though she was still unemployed.

Lian could afford the COBRA premiums because she had maximized her HSA balance, and the COBRA premiums for an HDHP plan are lower than for a traditional low-deductible health plan.

When can contributions be made?

Eligibility is determined on a monthly basis

Eligibility to contribute to an HSA is determined on a monthly basis.

- Participants must be enrolled in a qualified HDHP on the first day of the month in order to make or receive an HSA contribution during that month (IRC Sec. 223(c)(1)(A)).

- Unless you are contributing under the full-contribution rule (see the previous section), you cannot make HSA contributions for the months you are not covered by an HDHP.

Contributions are tied to the tax year

Contributions are reported on the individual tax return and are therefore tied to the tax return for that year. Consequently, the contribution may not be made before the beginning of the tax year that it covers, and it must be made no later than the legal deadline, without extensions, for filing the individual's income tax return for that year (IRS Notice 2004-2 Q&A 21).

Most individuals are calendar-year taxpayers. For such individuals, contributions can be made between January 1 of a given year and April 15 of the following year.

Even though your health coverage plan year may be any 12-month period established by an employer or insurer for managing the plan and accounting for benefit payments, the schedule for HSA contributions aligns with the tax year.

Timing of contributions

You have a lot of flexibility in deciding when to make your contributions. You and your employer can make your contributions in one or more payments at any time of the tax year, according to your convenience.

Example
Front-loading the HSA early in the year
Miles and Donetta knew their first baby was going to be born early in the year with a gastrointestinal defect that would probably require him to spend his first few weeks in the neonatal intensive care unit.

The hospital told them that they would be responsible for paying their entire out-of-pocket maximum immediately following their child's birth. If they did not have enough money in their HSA, then they would be making those payments with post-tax dollars.

Donetta and the baby were healthy enough that she could keep working until a month before the baby's birth.

She and Miles decided to have her entire paycheck deposited into their HSA. When they had contributed up to the $7,000 family limit for 2019, they stopped the HSA payroll deductions.

When the baby was born, they paid their deductible and coinsurance out of the HSA until their out-of-pocket maximum was met. Then their HDHP paid 100 percent of their remaining expenses.

Miles calculated their tax savings and the credit interest rates they avoided. He estimated that their actual out-of-pocket expense was much lower than it would have been had they been enrolled in their previous traditional low-deductible, PPO plan.

Transfers from other tax-advantaged accounts

Transferring an HSA from one trustee to another

Trustee-to-trustee transfers are transfers of account balances directly from one trustee or custodian to another.

Transfers from other HSAs or from Archer MSAs into an HSA are permitted, as long as the primary account holder is the same for both accounts (IRS Notice 2002-4 Q&A 23).

You may not transfer money from another individual's HSA—even if they are a family member or spouse—into an HSA in your name.

HSA transfers of balances accumulated in previous tax years do not affect the current year's contribution limits. This type of transfer is similar to moving funds from one IRA to another.

There is no limit to the number of trustee-to-trustee transfers you can make within a 12-month period.

Rollover contributions from another HSA or MSA

Rollover contributions are moving the funds from one HSA or Archer MSA to another, but the funds are sent to the account holder rather than directly from one trustee/custodian to another. The individual then has 60 days to get the funds back into an HSA without incurring taxes or penalties.

Only one rollover can be completed in a 12-month period. Just like trustee-to-trustee transfers, the rollover does not apply toward the contribution limits for the year

(IRC Sec. 223(f)(5)) (IRS Notice 2004-50 Q&A 55).

Example

Transferring an HSA to another bank or trustee

Tyler has an HSA with $5,000 at Bank A, and he wishes to transfer the entire balance to an HSA at Bank B.

He can rollover his money by withdrawing the balance from Bank A and re-depositing it into Bank B, as long as it is done within 60 days (he may also request a trustee-to-trustee transfer, in which Bank A sends the money directly to Bank B).

Tyler may choose either of these options and still make whatever contributions he is eligible to make for that tax year, without having to consider the rolled over amount in his yearly limit calculations.

However, if Tyler withdraws the money and does not re-deposit it or spend it for qualified healthcare within 60 days, a 20 percent penalty will apply and he will have to pay income tax on the amount withdrawn (IRC Sec. 223(f)(4)).

IRA transfers (IRC Sec. 223(b)(4)(C), 408(d)(9); IRS Notice 2008-51)

To help fund the HSA, an account holder can do a once-per-lifetime trustee-to-trustee transfer from a traditional or Roth IRA to the HSA. This transfer is limited to the maximum annual contribution for the year, and it reduces the annual amount that can be otherwise contributed.

The individual must remain an eligible individual for the entire 12-month testing period following the month the transfer is completed. If he or she does not remain eligible, the transferred amount is included as income for tax purposes and is assessed an additional 10 percent penalty.

Simple and SEP IRAs are not eligible for transfer.

Contributions by spouses

An HSA is an individual account only. Even when a husband and wife work for the same employer, their HSAs and contributions must be separate. Spouses cannot combine their HSAs into one joint account.

The rules for married people apply only if both spouses are eligible individuals. Contribution limits for spouses depend on the kind of coverage each spouse chooses.

- If either spouse has family HDHP coverage, then both spouses are treated as having family HDHP coverage (IRC Sec. 223(b)(5)(A)).

- If each spouse has family coverage under a separate plan, then the contribution limit for the two of them combined is $7,000 in 2019. The contribution limit is split equally between the spouses, unless they agree on a different division (IRC Sec. 223(b)(5)(B)(ii);IRS Notice 2004-50 Q&A 32).

- If both spouses are 55 or older and not enrolled in Medicare, then each spouse's contribution limit is increased by the $1,000 catch-up contribution. If both spouses meet the age requirement, the total contributions under family coverage cannot be more than $9,000 ($7,000 + $1,000 + $1,000) in 2019. Each spouse must make the catch-up contribution to his or her own HSA.

Example

Both spouses have family coverage

Tom, age 58, and Alice, age 53, are married.

Tom and Alice each have family coverage under a separate HDHP.

Because both plans provide family coverage, Tom and Alice are treated as having coverage under one family plan.

If they decide to split the $7,000 maximum family contribution for 2019 equally, Tom can contribute a total of $4,500 to his HSA (half of the annual statutory amount of $7,000 for 2019, plus a $1,000 catch-up contribution because he is over 55).

Alice can contribute $3,500 to her HSA (half of the $7,000 annual maximum for a family). Being only 53, she is not eligible to make an additional catch-up contribution.

Tom and Alice can agree to contribute different amounts, but their total annual 2019 contributions cannot exceed $8,000 ($7,000 + $1,000).

Example

Both spouses have self-only coverage

Jim, age 35, and Kathy, age 33, are married. Each has a self-only HDHP, and each has an HSA.

Jim can contribute $3,500 to his HSA in 2019, and Kathy can contribute $3,500 to her HSA.

The same applies whether Jim and Kathy work for different employers, one is self-employed and one is an employee, or both are self-employed.

Example

One spouse has qualifying coverage, the other does not

David and Sherry are married. David's employer offers an HSA-qualified HDHP. Sherry's employer offers a traditional PPO plan that does not meet eligibility requirements for an HDHP.

Sherry elects family coverage, thereby covering David under her non-qualifying plan. David is not eligible to contribute to an HSA, because he is covered under Sherry's traditional plan.

However, if Sherry elected coverage under her plan for solely herself or their children included, David would not be covered under her plan. He could participate in his employer's HSA-qualified HDHP instead and contribute to his own HSA.

Example

One spouse is eligible to contribute to an HSA, the other is not

Joe, age 65, and Jenny, age 56, are married. Joe recently turned 65 and enrolled in Medicare.

Joe and Jenny have separate HSAs, each with self-only coverage.

Joe can no longer contribute to his HSA, but can continue to use the funds accumulated in his account or Jenny's account to pay qualified medical expenses. He can also use his HSA to pay his Medicare premiums (IRC 223(d)(2)(C)(iv), IRS Notice 2004-2 Q&A 27, IRS Notice 2004-50 Q&A 4 and 45, and IRS Notice 2008-59 Q&A 29). However, he cannot use Jenny's HSA for his Medicare premiums because Jenny has not reached age 65 (IRS Notice 2008-59 Q&A 30).

Jenny is enrolled in a qualified HDHP. She is eligible to contribute up to $3,500 to her HSA in 2019, plus a catch-up contribution of $1,000, because she is older than 55.

Example
Family and single coverage at the same time
Al and Sue are married.

Because he has young children from a previous marriage, Al has a family HDHP with a $5,000 deductible. Through her employer, Sue has a self-only HDHP with a $2,000 deductible.

Because one spouse has a family HDHP that could potentially cover the other spouse, they are seen as having family coverage. Their maximum combined contribution is the IRS statutory amount for family coverage—$7,000 for 2019, to be divided between them by agreement.

They file separate tax returns. Because she has no children of her own to claim as deductions like Al does, they determine that they could save the most on taxes if Sue makes a larger contribution toward the HSA. They decide that Sue will contribute 75 percent of the yearly maximum HSA contribution for their family ($5,250), and Al will contribute 25 percent ($1,750).

Contributions by an individual or a sole proprietor

Sole proprietors are treated the same as individuals who make their own HSA contributions. They can deduct their own HSA contributions and health insurance payments from their personal income tax returns.

Sole proprietors cannot deduct their own HSA contributions as a business expense. However, amounts contributed on behalf of their employees may be deductible on Schedule C. The owner's HSA contribution is not a deduction attributable to the self-employed individual's trade or business, so it is not taken as a deduction on Schedule C, nor is it taken into account in determining net earnings from self-employment on Schedule SE (IRS Notice 2004-50 Q&A 84).

Contributions by a partnership and multiple member LLCs

Contributions from a partnership to a partner's HSA are not contributions by an employer. These contributions are treated as a distribution of money to the partner.

Contributions from a partner to an HSA in exchange for services rendered are treated as guaranteed payments. They can be deducted by the partner and are included in the partner's gross income.

In both situations, the partner can deduct the contribution made to the HSA (See Rev. Rul. 91.26, IRC Section 707 and the regulations thereunder).

Contributions by an S corporation

Contributions by an S corporation to a greater than two percent shareholder/employee's HSA for services rendered are treated as guaranteed payments, are deducted by the S corporation, and are included in the shareholder-employee's gross income. The shareholder employee can deduct the contribution made to the shareholder/employee's HSA on his or her personal income tax return (greater than two percent shareholders are treated as self-employed individuals. See above regarding rules on guaranteed payments for partners. Single member LLCs are treated the same as sole proprietors).

Penalties for contributing too much to your HSA

Excess contribution

If you contribute more than the allowable amount to your HSA for the tax year, it is called an excess contribution. Excess contributions are included in income and subject to a six percent excise tax. Excess employer contributions also become subject to income and federal excise tax.

You can avoid paying the excise tax and withdraw some or all of the excess contributions if you meet the following conditions:

- You withdraw the excess contributions by the due date of your tax return for the year the contributions were made.

- You withdraw any income earned on the withdrawn contributions and include the earnings in "other income" on your tax return for the year you withdraw the contributions and earnings (IRC Sec. 223(f)(3), IRS Notice 2004-2 Q&A 22).

Failing the testing period under the full-contribution rule

If you used the full-contribution rule to make a full year's allowable contribution to your HSA, but you did not fulfill the testing period, the penalty is a 10 percent tax, plus income tax on the over-contribution.

If you find out that you will not meet the testing period before the tax filing deadline for the previous year, you can follow the steps for withdrawing excess contributions in the section above.

If you lose your eligibility after the previous year's tax filing deadline, you must follow the steps earlier in the chapter under the section, 'Contributing under the full-contribution rule" to calculate the additional tax you will need to pay on your over-contribution.

Calculating penalties for excess contributions

The most reliable way to determine your tax liability for excess contributions is to download IRS Form 5329 and read its instructions from www.irs.gov to use the form as a worksheet.

CHAPTER 5
Using and growing your HSA

Whose expenses can your HSA cover?

Under the law, HSA distributions are tax-free if used for qualified medical expenses for:

- You and your spouse
- Any dependents you claim on your tax return
- Any person you could have claimed as a dependent on your tax return

Whose expenses does your HSA cover?

Under the law, HSA distributions are tax-free if used for qualified medical expenses for:

You and your spouse

This is true whether or not your spouse or dependent is covered by an HDHP. Even if both spouses have an HSA, one spouse can pay for qualified medical expenses for the other.

Any dependents you claim on your tax return

A person you claim as a dependent or qualifying child for income tax purposes must meet each of the following criteria (IRC Sec. 152, IRS Notice 2008-5):

- Bears a relationship to the taxpayer in one of the following ways:
    - A child (including a legally adopted or foster child), grandchild or great-grandchild
    - A stepchild or your stepchild's descendant
    - A sibling, half-sibling, step-sibling, or a descendant of these
    - A parent, grandparent, or other direct blood ancestor
    - A stepfather or stepmother
    - A brother or sister of your father or mother
    - A descendant of your brother or sister
    - A father-in-law, mother-in-law, son-in-law, daughter-in-law, brother-in-law or sister-in-law

- The qualifying child has a gross income for the calendar year that is less than the exemption amount allowed for the tax year by the IRS.

- The qualifying child must derive over one-half of his or her support for the calendar year from the taxpayer (special rules may apply to children of divorce, children with disabilities or other situations).

- The qualifying child must meet certain age requirements. He or she must be under 19 or under 24 if a full-time student.

- He or she cannot be a qualifying child of another taxpayer for the taxable year.

Special rule for HSA: An individual can be treated as a dependent for qualified medical expenses even if:
- The person filed a joint return.
- The person had a gross income of 4,000 or more.
- You or your spouse, if filing jointly, can be claimed as a dependent on someone else's return (IRC Sec. 223(d)(2)(A), IRS Notice 2008-59 Q&A 33, IRS Pub 969).

Example

Paying expenses for a spouse who is not covered by an HDHP

Sherry has a traditional plan that does not meet the criteria for an HDHP and does not cover David, her husband.

Sherry's plan has first-dollar coverage that is subject to co-payments. David elects an HDHP and HSA for himself.

Even though Sherry is not covered by David's HDHP, he can use his HSA to pay for her co-payments (IRS Notice 2004-50 Q&A 36).

Multiple definitions of dependent

The word "dependent" is used differently in PPACA (healthcare reform law) than in the IRS tax code. Health plans and state laws add confusion with their own rules for dependents.

For making qualified distributions from an HSA, a dependent is defined by the Internal Revenue Code (IRC), Section 152, and is explained in more detail in the previous section.

Adult children up to age 26

PPACA requires that health plans offer coverage for adult children up to age 26 under a parent's family health plan. While they may qualify as a dependent for insurance purposes, adult children might not qualify as tax dependents on the parent's tax return. If that is the case, their medical expenses cannot be covered by a parent's HSA (IRC sec. 152, 223(d)(2); PHS Sec. 2714).

However, an adult child who is covered under a parent's family HSA-eligible HDHP but is not a tax dependent can open his or her own HSA and contribute up to the full family maximum.

Same-sex spouses

HSAs can be used to pay medical expenses of same-sex spouses. As of June 25, 2015, under Obergefell v Hodges, the Supreme Court of the United States ruled that all states must recognize same sex marriage. HealthEquity's interpretation is that for federal income and state tax purposes there is no difference between spouses and same-sex spouses. For federal tax purposes, domestic partners are not considered spouses (IRS Notice 2014-1).

Paying for qualified medical expenses

Your HSA can be used for a wide variety of medical expenses, including those which are deducted from your individual tax return if you are eligible (see Appendix C for a detailed list of qualified medical expenses).

Any money from the HSA used for non-medical purposes will be included in the individual's gross income for tax purposes and is subject to an additional 20 percent penalty on the amount included (IRC Sec. 223(f)(4)(A)). However, if the account holder or beneficiary reaches age 65, distributions may be used for other purposes without being subject to the penalty. Income taxes will still apply (IRC Sec. 223(f)(4)(B) and (C)).

When must expenses be incurred?

Only expenses incurred after you establish your HSA are considered qualified. Expenses incurred before you establish your HSA are not qualified medical expenses (IRS Notice 2004-50 Q&A-39).

When is an HSA established?

Under federal law, you cannot contribute to an HSA or incur qualified expenses until the first day of the month after you enroll in a qualified HDHP. If you enroll in your HDHP on the first day of a month, you can open your HSA that same day.

State trust law determines when an HSA is established (IRS Notice 2008-59 Q&A 38). In most cases, it can be as soon as you complete your account application, pass the Consumer Identity Program (CIP) verification required by the Patriot Act, and fund your account.

An HSA that is funded by amounts which have rolled over from an Archer MSA or other HSA is established on the date the prior account was established.

If, under the full-contribution rule, you are considered eligible for the entire year for determining the contribution amount, only the expenses incurred after you establish your HSA are qualified medical expenses.

Some state laws (e.g., Utah) have determined that an HSA is deemed open on the first day that the tax payers are considered covered by a qualified HDHP. Check with your tax professional for more details.

IRC definition of qualified medical expenses

Appendix C has a detailed list of qualified medical expenses. Here are some general guidelines from IRS Publication 502:

- Medical expenses are the costs of diagnosis, cure, mitigation, treatment or prevention of disease, and the costs for treatments affecting any part or function of the body (IRC Sec. 213(d)).

- Medical expenses include payments for legal medical services rendered by physicians, surgeons, dentists and other medical practitioners. They also include the costs of equipment, supplies and diagnostic devices needed for these purposes.

- Medical care expenses must be primarily used to alleviate or prevent a physical or mental defect or illness. They do not include expenses that are merely beneficial to general health, such as vitamins (unless prescribed) or a vacation.

- Medical expenses include the premiums for long-term care insurance, COBRA premiums and insurance premiums paid during periods of unemployment. Other long-term care expenses beyond premiums can also be paid from an HSA.

Paying for some insurance premiums

(IRC Sec. 223(d)(2)(C); IRS Notice 2004-2 Q&A 27; IRS Notice 2005-59 Q&A 29)

Generally, you cannot use your HSA to pay medical insurance premiums, but there are some exceptions.

Medicare premiums

Once you are 65 and eligible for Medicare, you can use your HSA to pay Medicare premiums (A, B, C, and D), out-of-pocket expenses that Medicare does not pay, and Medicare HMO premiums.

You cannot pay Medigap premiums with your HSA. Medigap is insurance that individuals can buy to cover out-of-pocket costs that are not covered by Medicare.

Premiums for employer-based coverage after age 65

If you are 65 or older and still work, you can pay your share of premiums for employer-based coverage out of your HSA (you cannot pay for these premiums before age 65).

If you are 65 or older and do not work, you can pay your share of any premiums your employer requires you to pay from your HSA for employer-sponsored retiree healthcare coverage.

Premiums when you are unemployed

You can pay for healthcare coverage while receiving unemployment compensation under federal or state law.

You can also pay COBRA premiums with HSA dollars if you are eligible for COBRA benefits.

Long-term care insurance

You may use your HSA to pay premiums for qualified long-term care insurance. To be qualified, a long-term care insurance plan must meet criteria determined by federal law (see IRS Publication 969).

Restrictions your HSA trustee or custodian may impose

It is your responsibility to prove that you have spent your HSA funds in accordance with the law. However, the trustee or custodian can limit your access to HSA distributions under certain conditions.

For example, the trustee may prohibit distributions for amounts less than $50, or may only allow a certain number of distributions.

Trustees and custodians may impose different restrictions (including no restrictions at all) on distributions. If easy access to your account is important to you, consider this feature when shopping for an HSA.

Paying for services covered under your health plan

In general, the HSA-qualified HDHP combination is the most flexible type of healthcare arrangement available. The money in the HSA is yours to spend and save. This means you can choose to obtain treatment from virtually any licensed provider of qualified medical services, whether they are in or out of your network, as long as you are willing to pay with your HSA.

Using network providers

Your HSA money typically goes further if you take advantage of the discounts provided by your health plan's network.

Healthcare providers—doctors, hospitals and other healthcare facilities—participating in your plan's network have agreed to give members of your plan a discount on their usual charges.

Depending on your plan's rules, you may also need to use a gatekeeper or primary care physician to obtain referrals and authorizations for certain medical services or procedures in order to get the best benefits your plan offers.

A gatekeeper physician is usually a primary care doctor, pediatrician or internist who is responsible for overseeing and coordinating all aspects of a patient's care.

A referral is a recommendation from one physician to see another physician, usually a specialist. In many managed care plans, in order for the service to be covered, a referral may be necessary to see any practitioner or specialist other than your gatekeeper physician.

An authorization is the health plan's permission to proceed with a medical or surgical procedure. Like a referral, an authorization may be required if you want the plan to pay for the procedure. Without authorization, the plan may refuse to pay for the procedure, even if the procedure might have otherwise been covered.

A managed care plan is a health plan that limits the reimbursement levels paid to providers by monitoring healthcare utilization of participants.

If you use your HSA only for services covered under your plan and consult only providers who participate in your plan's network, all of your expenditures under the HSA will generally count toward your deductible and toward your plan's out-of-pocket limits.

Example

Paying a network provider

Maria's doctor charges $150 for a visit for an acute sore throat.

As a provider in her health plan's network, her doctor has agreed to accept $75 from her plan for this type of visit.

Maria does not pay her provider the $150 charge at the time of the visit. Because her provider is in her plan's network, she waits for the claim to be repriced after the health plan applies the discount that her provider agreed to accept. She may also receive a bill directly from her doctor for the adjusted amount.

If she has not yet met her deductible at the time of the visit, she pays the $75 out of her HSA or out of her other savings with post-tax dollars.

This amount is also credited toward her plan's annual out-of-pocket limit, or limit on how much she can expect to spend in a given year before the plan takes over entirely.

Even if you use network providers, you still need to understand exactly how your plan expects you to obtain care. Your plan may require you to obtain a referral to see a specialist or authorization for a medical procedure, even if the specialist or the doctor recommending the procedure participates in your plan.

If you fail to obtain a referral or authorization when one is required, your plan may charge you a higher co-payment, coinsurance rate or a flat-dollar penalty. The excess co-payments, coinsurance or penalties for not using network providers will not count toward your HDHP's out-of-pocket limit for the year; however, you will be able to pay these out of your HSA.

Failure to know and follow your plan's rules can cost you money.

Separate out-of-pocket limits for out-of-network care

HSA law permits health plans to have separate out-of-pocket limits for out-of-network care.

Refusal of charges

If your provider has not contracted with your plan, then the plan is not obligated to accept the provider's full charges.

Plans typically count only what they consider usual, customary and reasonable (UCR). UCR is the estimated "going rate" paid in your geographical area for a given medical service or procedure. This amount is credited toward the participant's deductible and out-of-pocket limits.

Example

Only a portion of a provider's fees are applied to the deductible

Maria's doctor charges $150 for a sore throat evaluation. Her insurance company decides that the usual and customary charge is $130. It then pays half of this reduced amount.

Maria pays the remaining half, and possibly an additional $20 if the doctor does not have a previous agreement to accept the plan's reduced charges and passes them on to Maria directly.

If this happens, Maria's cost for the visit is $85. The doctor still gets paid his usual charge of $150—$85 from Maria and $65 from her insurance company.

However, because her insurance company has not allowed the full amount of her doctor's charges to be considered, only $65 of the $85 she paid is credited toward her deductible and out-of-pocket limit for the year.

Paying for services not covered under your health plan

You can use your HSA balance to pay for healthcare not covered under your health plan within the limits of qualified expenses. This includes many dental and vision expenses, as well as many less-common expenses such as removing lead-based paint from your residence.

However, because removing lead-based paint is an expense that would generally not be covered by a health insurance plan, that kind of expense would not be applied toward your health plan deductible. See Appendix C for more details.

Methods of payment from an HSA

The basic process of paying for care under an HSA is much the same as it is under other healthcare plans.

Traditional plan

In a traditional plan, you typically pay for care in one of two ways, depending on whether the doctor or other provider participates in your plan's network.

- **In-network care:** If the provider participates in your network, you typically present your healthcare plan membership card and pay the required co-payment at the time of the visit. The provider files your claim with the insurance company and gets paid the contractually agreed or repriced amount. If there is also coinsurance that is applicable to the service, then the provider bills you for the balance due.

- **Out-of-network care:** If the provider does not participate in your plan's network, the process is different. You pay the entire bill at the time of the visit, because an out-of-network provider typically will not submit the claim to your plan for you. Then you may be reimbursed by your insurance company for part of what you paid, depending on how much of your deductible, if any, has been met for the year.

HSA-qualified HDHP

With an HSA-qualified HDHP, the payment process at the doctor's office (hospital, laboratory or other facility) is similar.

Your HSA administrator may supply you with an HSA debit card, checkbook or both. They may also provide an online bill pay service that lets you pay providers directly from your HSA.

In-network care:

- If the doctor or provider is in your network or the service is for preventive care, you may not have to pay anything at the time you receive care, depending on the structure of your plan.

- The provider may ask you to pay part of the bill at the time of your visit. If possible, do not pay the entire bill since it has not been repriced and you might be overcharged. Also, remember that under PPACA, preventive care should be paid for by your health plan and not out of your HSA.

- After you have received care, the provider will submit your claim for repricing to the health plan. The health plan will pay its contractually agreed amount if you have met your deductible for the plan year. Additionally, the health plan takes into account whether you have a network discount, if the claim is for preventive care, and the amount you pay if you have not met your deductible.

- Depending on how your HSA is set up, you can pay your portion, if any, out of your bank account and file a claim for reimbursement from your HSA, or pay the amount directly out of your HSA using your HSA's online bill pay system.

Out-of-network care:

- If your provider does not participate in your plan's network, you may be required to pay at the time the care is provided. This also happens in a traditional plan. You can pay the expense out of your bank account or with a credit card and file a claim for reimbursement request from your HSA, or pay the amount directly out of your HSA using your HSA debit card or check.

- If you have overpaid the physician out of your HSA, you will receive a reimbursement that should be re-deposited into your HSA to avoid additional taxes.

Important strategies for managing payments to providers

While the basic outlines of the payment process are primarily the same whether you are enrolled in a traditional plan or in an HSA-qualified HDHP, it may be helpful to understand a few terms and steps in the payment process.

Be ready to pay co-payments and coinsurance or encounter fees

Most healthcare providers are not accustomed to cashless visits—where the patient is not expected to pay something at the time of the visit.

In a traditional plan, your co-payment or coinsurance is your part of the bill for care and the balance comes from your plan.

To accommodate the needs of providers, some HSA-qualified HDHPs may provide for an encounter fee, or an amount you pay at the time of a visit. While this fee may not represent your full financial responsibility to the provider, it is counted toward your financial responsibility for that visit and for your annual care.

Try not to pay retail price for visits

Important: Many providers, both in- and out-of-network, are unfamiliar with HSA-qualified HDHPs, and they will try to charge you retail price when you receive services. Speak with your HSA provider or health plan about the best way to obtain fair pricing when you visit your doctor.

Build your HSA early in the year

The law governing HSAs provides you and your employer with a good amount of flexibility in funding your HSA. You or your employer can make contributions to the HSA on any schedule that is convenient, as long as the total contributions made to your account in a given year do not exceed the annual maximum contribution limits. Best of all, unlike most FSAs, funds in your HSA are not "use-it-or-lose-it", so you do not need to worry about forfeiting unspent dollars.

If you have a bill that exceeds your balance, you can pay the bill using other resources, then file for reimbursement from your HSA once your balance has grown sufficiently. Your HSA trustee will provide you with forms or another process for reimbursements.

Duplicate reimbursements must be returned to the HSA

If you pay directly from the HSA and then receive a duplicate reimbursement from the insurance company, the reimbursed amount must be returned to the HSA administrator as a mistaken distribution. If you do not return the duplicate reimbursement, you will have to pay a penalty to the IRS. This also applies to any refunds you receive from health providers for over-payment.

Mistaken distributions from an HSA can be repaid by April 15—or other date designated by the IRS—of the following year without penalty or tax, provided this is permitted by the trustee, and there is "convincing evidence that the amounts were distributed from an HSA because of a mistake of fact due to reasonable cause" (IRS Notice 2004-50 Q&A 37).

Investing your HSA funds (IRS Notice 2004-50 Q&A 65)

If you make your annual maximum contributions, are careful with your funds and look for ways to get the best value (for example, comparing prescription prices at different pharmacies and using in-network providers), the money in your HSA will grow and earn interest over the years.

When your account balance reaches the minimum balance required by your HSA administrator for investing, you can invest any money over that threshold in HSA-qualified investment funds. Most HSA administrators provide a website that enables you to set up your investments and make trades.

Investment choices

HSAs can be invested in the same investments approved for IRAs—i.e. bank accounts, annuities, certificates of deposit (CDs), stocks, mutual funds or bonds. However, no part of the HSA trust assets can be invested in life insurance contracts, collectibles (art, antiques etc.—other tangible personal property that the IRS specifies), and HSA assets may not be co-mingled with other property except for investment purposes.

Earnings and risk

Earnings on money invested from your HSA accrue tax-free. However, all investments carry the same risk as the stock market and mutual funds and are not federally-insured.

Moving funds back into your HSA

If you have a large medical expense, you can move money out of your investments back into your HSA with no tax penalties and without affecting your yearly contribution maximum. If you choose an HSA administrator that offers no trading fees, you may also be able to make trades and maintain your investment account with no extra fees.

CHAPTER 6
Becoming a smart healthcare consumer

Getting the most out of your HSA

As you become more educated about how your health plan works and ways to manage the features of your HSA, you will be able to stretch the dollars in your account to cover more healthcare needs, or better yet, earn more interest.

Put premium savings into your HSA

A higher deductible generally means lower monthly premiums. Take this into account when deciding whether or not to choose an HSA-qualified HDHP option.

While it may seem intimidating to take on a high deductible, an HDHP can cost significantly less. You can deposit all or some of your premium savings into your HSA. The balance in your account can be used to offset the higher deductible. If you do not need the money for medical expenses, it can grow. Unlike premium expenses and FSA contributions which are "use it or lose it", you get to keep your HSA dollars.

Compare coinsurance and co-payment levels

Another way to balance the benefits and risks of an HSA is to understand coinsurance levels. Coinsurance and co-payments determine what you pay once you and your family reach your plan's deductible.

Different coinsurance and co-payment levels can affect the premium price and the additional amount you may need to pay out of your HSA or out-of-pocket once the deductible is met.

For example, if your coinsurance level is 100 percent (your plan pays 100 percent after the deductible), your premium will most likely be higher than one with a coinsurance of 80/20 (the plan pays 80 percent and you pay 20 percent until you meet your out-of-pocket maximum). Most coinsurance levels will vary for in- and out-of-pocket network care.

Take advantage of your HRA or FSA

Some employers offer limited-purpose HRAs to cover the gap between your deductible and the out-of-pocket maximum. Study the requirements for this benefit, keep good records of your expenses and watch the calendar. Many people neglect to submit reimbursement requests to their employers before the FSA's or HRA's run-out deadline.

You may also have a limited-purpose FSA in conjunction with an HSA. During your open enrollment period, talk to your dentist and vision services providers to get an estimate of the dental and vision care you will need, then make an election for an FSA contribution to cover that amount. Make sure you do not over-contribute to the FSA, because you can lose any unspent money at the end of the year. Using an FSA for your dental and vision expenses instead of your HSA lets you stretch your HSA balance further. Limited-purpose FSAs make the most sense for people who contribute the annual maximum to their HSA. You should always "top off" your HSA before contributing to your limited-purpose FSA because HSA dollars can also be used for dental and vision, but they are not "use it or lose it" accounts.

Watch out-of-pocket maximums

Maximum out-of-pocket costs for health plans that qualify for HSA eligibility for individuals ($6,650 for 2018 and $6,750 for 2019) and families ($13,300 for 2018 and $13,500 for 2019) are set by the IRS for in-network care.

However, HDHP plans can have higher out-of-pocket maximums for out-of-network care. To reduce costs, be sure you know how much you will pay for out-of-network care before committing to it. Your out-of-pocket maximum level can affect your exposure and your ability to go out-of-network to receive expensive care.

Determine the right amount of money to contribute to your HSA

Try to contribute the most money the law allows and that you are financially able to contribute to your HSA each year.

HSA tax benefits

HSAs have the best tax benefits of any savings accounts, including traditional IRAs, 401(k)s and Roth IRAs.

Only an HSA lets the owner make tax-deductible deposits, enjoy tax-free growth through interest or investments, and spend the money on qualified health-related services and products without paying taxes.

Unlike most other medical spending accounts such as FSAs or HRAs, the money in your HSA is yours to keep. It can also be used for non-health related costs by paying only your income tax, with no penalties, when you reach age 65.

Many people, including those with HSAs, may be on tight budgets and unable to fully fund the account. The good news is that the government allows you to make your contributions throughout the year until April 15 (or an IRS-adjusted date) of the following year and still receive tax benefits.

Funding strategies for HSAs and 401(k)s

Many employers are now offering their employees access to both 401(k)s and HSAs. Employees that fund both of these accounts should consider the unique triple-tax advantaged benefits of the HSA as they decide upon their funding strategy. You should consider funding these accounts in the following order:

- First, consider funding either or both accounts to optimize any available employer matching contributions that are available.
- After you have taken advantage of employer matching, fund the HSA to the allowable annual maximum.
- Then fund the 401(k) to the allowable annual maximum.

Consider this order of funding to benefit from employer matching funds while protecting your money from avoidable taxes. Remember, the HSA does not have FICA (social security) taxes on contributions and avoids taxes when you spend the dollars on qualified healthcare.

Use payroll deductions to prefund your account for anticipated expenses

If you expect a large medical expense during the year, try to put your money into your HSA first through an increased payroll deduction, instead of paying directly out-of-pocket. That way, you can pay with pre-tax dollars. This increases the value of your money (depending on your tax bracket) by 18 percent to 30 percent.

You can also fully fund your HSA at the beginning of the year as long as you are covered by a qualified HDHP for the entire year.

Example

Funding the HSA early in the year for an anticipated medical expense

The Jensen family is expecting their second child in July, and their HDHP plan year began on January 1, 2018.

They have family coverage with a $5,000 deductible and no embedded deductible. Their plan has maternity coverage and no coinsurance once the deductible is met.

Expecting out-of-pocket expenses in July associated with the birth of their child, they increased their HSA contributions to $800 per month, so that by July 1, they will have deposited $4,800 in their HSA for the year.

For the 2018 tax year, the Jensens can deposit up to $6,900 into their account, so they can still contribute $2,100 over the next six months, assuming they remain eligible to contribute to the HSA for the entire year.

When they receive bills for the birth, they will have money in their HSA to satisfy up to $5,000 in bills.

Costs exceeding $5,000 will be fully paid by the HDHP, provided they remain in-network.

Consider hospital indemnity plans and other gap coverage

The HSA law allows you to use other types of insurance with your HDHP that can help offset the risk that comes with a higher deductible.

These policies include homeowner's insurance, automobile insurance, dental and vision care plans, accidental injury insurance, workers' compensation benefits, hospital indemnity plans that pay a fixed amount per day of hospitalization, and specific disease policies that pay a fixed amount for the designated disease.

The permitted plans help preserve your HSA balance and protect you from out-of-pocket expenses (IRC Sec. 223(c)(3)(C)).

Become a careful shopper

The internet and your health plan should provide many opportunities to compare costs and shop for bargains on prescriptions and medical supplies. There are also some good websites that rate hospitals and compare costs of treatments. Your HSA administrator may provide links to cost comparison tools and websites on your HSA member portal. Spend time to become familiar with these resources.

You can also find suitable home-use alternatives to medications or supplies you usually get through your provider by comparison shopping at retail stores.

Example

Finding bargains on healthcare

Holly, age 35, is married and a mother of four. She was recently diagnosed with insulin-dependent diabetes.

Holly's husband recently left a job that offered health benefits through a low deductible, traditional plan. His new employer offers an HSA-qualified HDHP.

In Holly's words, "In a health insurance plan with a consistent co-payment of $10, I never had a reason to ask questions about the costs of services. I just paid the co-payment and felt grateful to have insurance pay the rest–or so I thought.

"Under my traditional HMO insurance plan, the pharmacy simply filled my prescriptions for my insulin and supplies, and I didn't see any need to look for more cost-effective prices. I was happy to pay my $35 co-payment for insulin.

"When introduced to health savings accounts, I was worried that I wouldn't get the same benefits. I learned, though, that not only did I receive comparable care, I also learned to be a careful shopper and save money.

"I began to ask questions about such things as lab work, blood tests and examinations. I learned how to save money by switching to generic drugs and buying a less expensive blood glucose monitor and test strips. I found out that the typical blood work done at my doctor's office cost anywhere from $55 to $70.

"I found out that I could buy my own hemoglobin A1C test at my pharmacy for about $24. I did the test at home and called my doctor with the results. I also learned to watch for coupons and rebates.

"I've become more of a researcher for myself and for my children. Before taking them to the doctor or to the urgent care, I go online to learn what I can about their symptoms and possible treatments.

"I've discovered that by controlling my own medical dollars, I'm more conscientious about what I'm doing and spending, and we have saved money."

Case studies

As you become familiar with the covered benefits, deductibles, contributions and out-of-pocket expenses associated with your HDHP, you can begin to understand and plan for how to make your HSA work for you.

The following examples of real-life scenarios show how HSAs can help decrease insurance premiums and build good healthcare consumer skills. These studies illustrate how to get the most out of your HSA by:

- Understanding and selecting the best HDHP design for your situation.
- Determining the right amount of money to contribute to your HSA.

To make it easier to compare money in versus money out in each of these case studies, the employee HSA contribution is $0.

Case study 1:

Bill and Tammy—some chronic illness

Bill and Tammy are middle-aged and starting to need care for chronic illnesses. During his employer's open enrollment period for 2019 benefits, Bill decides to use his and Tammy's medical history from 2018 to compare benefit options.

In 2017, Bill and Tammy took advantage of free preventive care screenings through their health plan. They were on regular medications for some mild chronic illness. They had only one urgent care visit during the year.

	Bill	**Tammy**
Age	58	57
Health	High cholesterol	Type 1 diabetic
Medications	Lipitor®, 10 mg daily	Insulin, daily
Healthcare utilization	1 urgent care visit for cut hand Regular doctor and preventive visits	Regular doctor and preventive visits

The moment of truth came when Bill totaled the premiums, medical expenses and his employer's contribution to the HSA.

Even though he did not meet the relatively high HDHP plan deductible and had to pay for medical expenses out of his HSA (and a little out of his own pocket after he depleted the HSA), the direct hit to his pocket was still $1,938 less under the HSA-qualified HDHP.

	PPO plan		HDHP/HSA plan	
Money in				
Employer HSA contributions		$0	$125 x 12 months	$1,500
Money out				
Annual premiums	$275 x 12 months	$3,300	$125 x 12 months	$1,500
Total provider visits	Co-pays	$115	Paid from HSA	$895
Total prescriptions	Co-pays	$140	Paid from HSA	$722
Money out subtotal		$3,555		$3,117
Less the HSA employer contribution		$0		-$1,500
Total money out		$3,555		$1,617
Difference between PPO and HDHP/HSA money out				$1,938 savings
HSA balance remaining		$0		$0

Becoming a smart healthcare consumer | 89

Case study 2:

Julie—excellent health

Julie knows the importance of health insurance and good habits. She watches what she eats and gets enough exercise and sleep.

She has a relatively low income and she is very cost-sensitive.

	Julie
Age	35
Health	Excellent
Medications	1 generic prescription for strep
Healthcare utilization	2 doctor visits: Annual checkup Strep throat

Like Bill, Julie compares her two plan options using her expenses from 2018.

Julie is very concerned about the high deductible in the HSA-qualified HDHP. The $0 deductible in the PPO is very attractive to her. Even though she is in great health, she feels she cannot afford to cover unanticipated medical expenses. She does not have much money in her bank account at the end of each month.

She also sees that the out-of-pocket maximum for the HDHP is $3,000, compared to the $2,000 from the PPO plan.

Her employer is contributing $750 to her HSA, but she does not see much of an impact from that at first.

Insurance plan

	PPO plan		HDHP/HSA plan	
Deductible		$0		$1,500
Out-of-pocket maximum		$2,000		$3,000
Annual premiums	$85 x 12 months	$1,020	$25 x 12 months	$300
Employer HSA contributions		$0	$62.50 x 12 months	$750
Employee HSA contributions		n/a	$0 x 12 = $0	$0

Julie had her annual checkup, which was covered as a preventive benefit under her insurance plan.

Provider visits

	PPO plan		HDHP/HSA plan	
Annual preventive exam	Preventive covered at 100%	$0	Preventive covered at 100%	$0
$100 doctor visit for strep throat	$15 co-pay	$15	Pays from HSA	$100
Total provider costs		**$15**		**$100**

Becoming a smart healthcare consumer

Case study 2: (continued)

Julie's only prescription in 2018 was a generic medication for strep throat.

Prescriptions

	PPO plan		HDHP/HSA plan
$25 generic	$10 co-pay	$10	$25.00
Total prescriptions		$10	$25.00

Everything comes into perspective when Julie compares money in and money out. Between the low premium and her employer's contribution to her HSA, she would be much better off with an HSA-qualified HDHP.

While she had been worried about a high deductible and a high out-of-pocket maximum, in reality she finished the year with a positive balance of more than $600 in her HSA. With its $0 deductible, the PPO plan would have taken over $700 more out of her pocket compared to the HSA plan when she counts monthly premiums and co-pay costs.

	PPO plan		HDHP/HSA plan	
Money in				
Employer HSA contributions		$0	$62.50 x 12 months	$750
Money out				
Annual premiums	$85 x 12 months	$1,020	$25 x 12 months	$300
Total provider costs	Co-pays	$15	Paid from HSA	$100
Total prescriptions	Co-pays	$10	Paid from HSA	$25.00
Total money out		$1,045		$425.00
Difference between PPO and HDHP/HSA money out				$620.00 savings
HSA balance remaining		$0		$625.00

Case study 3:

The Walkers—accidental injuries

The Walkers have two children. Derek works for an electrical contractor and Lauren works at a local university. Lauren has better benefits, so the family is going to be covered by a family plan from her employer.

They have two very active, adventurous boys. One was injured in a bicycle accident in 2018. They have no reason to expect that the boys will become more cautious in 2019.

	Derek	**Lauren**	**Two children**
Age	38	36	10 and 6
Health	Excellent	Excellent	One child injured in a bicycle accident
Medications	None	None	None
Healthcare utilization	Regular doctor and preventive visits	Regular doctor and preventive visits	Regular doctor and preventive visits Hospital emergency room, surgery, and 3-day stay for injured child

Lauren compares her two 2019 plan options using the family's 2018 medical expenses as a guide. There is a PPO plan with a relatively low deductible and out-of-pocket maximum.

For family coverage, the HSA-qualified HDHP option has a higher deductible and out-of-pocket maximum.

Insurance plan

	PPO plan		HDHP/HSA plan	
Deductible		$250		$3,000
Maximum out-of-pocket limit		$2,500		$5,000
Coinsurance		20%		20%
Annual premiums	$170.75 x 12 months	$2,049	$0 x 12 months	$0
Employer HSA contributions		$0	$150 x 12 months	$1,800
Employee HSA contributions		n/a	$0 x 12 = $0	$0

The hospital expenses for one of her boys far exceeded the out-of-pocket maximum for both plans. So she just used the out-of-pocket amounts to compare the actual costs of each plan.

Provider visits

	PPO plan		HDHP/HSA plan	
Two annual preventive exams	Preventive covered at 100 percent	$0	Preventive covered at 100 percent	$0
Emergency room, surgery, labs, and prescriptions for bicycle accident	All expenses above out-of-pocket maximum paid 100 percent by health plan	$19,735	All expenses above out-of-pocket maximum paid 100 percent by health plan	$19,735
Out-of-pocket maximum	Entire amount paid out-of-pocket	$2,500	$1,800 paid from HSA; $3,200 paid out of pocket	$5,000

Becoming a smart healthcare consumer | 95

Case study 3: (continued)

When Lauren compared money in versus money out, she saw that the HSA-qualified HDHP option gave her family significantly more protection against true out-of-pocket expenses.

	PPO plan		HDHP/HSA plan	
Money in				
Employer HSA contributions		$0	$150 x 12 months	$1,800
Money out				
Annual premiums	$170.75 x 12 months	$2,049	$0 x 12 months	$0
Total provider costs		$2,500		$5,000
Money out subtotal		$4,549		$5,000
Less the HSA employer contribution		$0		$1800
Total money out		$4,549		$3,200
Difference between PPO and HDHP/HSA money out				$1,349 savings
HSA balance remaining		$0		$0

Lauren found that with this plan design, she was $1,349 better off by choosing the HDHP/HSA plan with a catastrophic scenario, and she would have been even better off if she had made additional pre-tax contributions to her HSA to pay for the added expenses.

CHAPTER 7
What if?

HSAs, medical procedures and life events

You may have your HSA for a long time. While you own it, you could experience many life events that affect your eligibility to have an HSA, the amount you can contribute, who your dependents are, what kinds of distributions you can make and whether you can have other kinds of health coverage.

This chapter describes the kind of decisions you might need to make and which actions to take should you face an unanticipated crisis or major life events—changes in employment, emergency and non-emergency medical issues, marriage or divorce, newborn or adopted children, disability, or death.

Medical procedures

What if I need surgery?

Imagine you have just been told you need surgery. If you understand your HSA-qualified HDHP, you can focus on making the best choices for your long-term medical and financial well-being.

Do your homework

Spend time researching your condition, the treatment possibilities, and the risks and benefits of certain treatments. Use the internet, visit a library and speak with friends and relatives who may have had a similar condition. Many HSA administrators and health plans offer powerful online tools that provide explanations, photographs and videos of possible treatments.

Get a second opinion

If you have been told you need surgery, get a second or third opinion as professionals often have different solutions to fix a health problem.

Most conditions can wait until you and your doctors understand your options. If you are facing major surgery, your HSA may be worth its weight in gold. You can use your HSA to get a second opinion from any expert you choose, whether or not that doctor is in your plan's network.

Even if you have not met your annual deductible, understand your plan's requirements concerning surgery. Many plans require you get authorization for non-emergency surgery and some may require a second opinion before authorization is given. Following the rules of your HDHP can cut waste, save money and allow you to use your HSA funds when you need them most.

Choose your doctor and hospital: The role of in-network providers

An HSA-qualified HDHP gives you the freedom to use either in-network or out-of-network providers. If you are facing a major medical event, such as surgery, you will want to fully explore the options in your network before proceeding.

Be sure you know whether your plan has separate out-of-pocket limits for in-network and out-of-network care, then decide whether you want to use a doctor or hospital in or out of your plan's network. If your plan has separate limits, you could wind up paying thousands of dollars more for care that is no better than what you would get from a provider in your network. Additionally, in-network providers will typically accept deeper discounts for care provided than out-of-pocket providers. This can also save you money.

If you do not have much money in your HSA, you may initially have to pay with after-tax dollars. Many hospitals and physicians accept payments over time. You can use future HSA deposits to make these payments, or to reimburse yourself if you pay the expenses with other funds. You will need to balance this benefit against any interest charges that the hospital or physician may add to your outstanding bill. Interest charges are not allowable HSA expenses.

If you are contemplating surgery, remember there will be many people involved in the procedure in addition to your principal surgeon. For example, the anesthesiologist should also be in your plan's network if you want the best benefits your plan offers. This is true if your plan has separate in- and out-of-network benefits.

Ask your doctor how many different specialists will be involved in your surgery and where your doctor has operating privileges. Then call the hospital and the other specialists and find out if they are part of your network. Your health plan also can provide this information by telephone or, usually, online. If the provider is not part of the network, they may be willing to give you a prompt-payment discount or honor your in-network pricing if you ask in advance. The time you take to explore these questions can save you a lot of money.

Authorizations and referrals

Make sure you know what your plan's requirements are concerning authorizations and referrals. Your plan may impose financial penalties if you do not get required referrals and authorizations, even if your provider is in your network. Penalties will not count toward meeting your out-of-pocket limit for the year. Choosing not to follow the plan's rules can cost you money.

Example

Negotiating discounts with an out-of-network provider

Heather is a 34-year-old mother of three who has been referred by her primary care physician to a surgeon for elective gallbladder removal due to pain and polyps.

The surgeon Heather has been referred to is not in her health plan's network. She feels comfortable with this surgeon and wants to use him anyway.

The surgeon's office explains that since Heather has an HSA and can pay promptly, they will offer a discounted fee, charging her only $50 more than a provider would charge in her network.

Heather then finds out that her out-of-network surgeon can perform surgery in both the out-of-network surgery center and the in-network hospital in her town.

Heather's surgeon agrees to schedule Heather's surgery at the in-network hospital, because this will save her significant out-of-pocket expenses.

Heather is willing to pay a little extra money in surgeon fees to have the gallbladder removal performed by the surgeon of her choice.

Because she is informed and selective, Heather saves potentially thousands of dollars by having her surgery performed at the in-network hospital.

What if I have a medical emergency?

An emergency is the sudden onset of a condition or an accidental injury requiring immediate medical or surgical care to avoid death or permanent disability.

Know your plan's rules about whom to call or visit in an emergency.

If you are having a life-threatening emergency, call 911 (in the US) and go to the nearest hospital.

Generally you, or a representative, such as a family member, must communicate with your plan within 24 to 48 hours of the onset of an emergency. However, if you are initially taken to an out-of-network facility, you do not have to change hospitals until your condition stabilizes.

As in the case of surgery, however, treatment of an emergency is likely to be expensive and you should consider using in-network providers once the danger period has passed.

If your situation is not life-threatening, you may want to call the health plan's urgent care line or nursing hotline before seeking care (the number is generally on the back of your health plan card).

An urgent condition is one that needs treatment within 24 hours to prevent it from turning into a serious or life-threatening illness. Calling first can be especially important if you are out-of-town, as the urgent care line personnel may be able to direct you to an urgent care center or hospital near you that is part of your plan's network (remember, many plans are national in scope and have in-network providers all over the country).

Using an in-network provider will save you money and stretch your HSA. If you are not sure whether your condition is urgent or an emergency, err on the side of caution, head for the emergency room first, and call later.

Other life events

What if I get married or add a child to my family?

If you get married, give birth, or adopt a child, your healthcare coverage needs may change. Under the Health Insurance Portability and Accountability Act (HIPAA), you have the right to ask your plan to cover new family member(s) without waiting until the plan's open enrollment period (see Appendix A for more information on HIPAA).

Enrolling a new spouse or baby in your plan

Enroll new family members in your plan as soon as possible. If you are changing from an individual plan to family coverage, your allowable HSA contribution will change on the first day of the first full month after which you elect a family-coverage HDHP, which will allow you to contribute more to your HSA. You may choose to make a prorated increase in your contributions for the year, or contribute the family maximum for the year if you believe you will stay in a family plan through the testing period.

Stepchildren

You can typically cover a stepchild in your employer's plan, even if you have not formally adopted the child. The child has to live with you in a parent-child relationship, and you have to be responsible for his or her support. Some plans require that you or your current spouse be able to claim the child as a dependent for tax purposes before allowing you to enroll the child in your plan.

As with adding a newborn, adding a stepchild to your plan may allow you to increase your HSA contribution. When determining the best way to cover a stepchild, consider the options under your plan, as well as those available if your spouse or partner has a different health plan.

Example

Conflict with spouse's family coverage may disqualify the HSA

Phil and Paula each have self-only coverage through their employers. Phil has an HSA-qualified HDHP, while Paula has a traditional plan with a low deductible that does not qualify as an HDHP.

Paula acquires custody of her daughter, Mary, who comes to live with them.

Paula wants to cover Mary under her plan. However, her plan only offers individual and family coverage. If she elects family coverage, Phil will no longer be able to contribute to an HSA, since he will be covered under her plan.

But if Phil's plan offers different options, such as self-plus-child, it may make sense for him to cover Mary under his plan.

What if my adult child becomes covered under my family HDHP?

The healthcare reform law (PPACA) extends parents' health insurance plan's dependent coverage to children until age 26, regardless of the child's marital status. However, the law does not require parents' insurance to cover dependents (spouse or children) of the adult child (the IRS definitions of dependent for healthcare coverage purposes are different. Make sure you consult your tax preparer for additional information).

If your adult child up to age 26 is covered by your family HDHP, but does not qualify as your tax dependent, the adult child can open his own HSA as long as he meets all other HSA eligibility requirements.

Your adult child does not have to split the maximum contribution limit for a family with you as you would with your spouse. He or she can contribute up to the full maximum family limit—$6,900 in 2018 and $7,000 in 2019. Additionally, your adult child's spouse and tax dependents can use the adult child's HSA for qualified medical expenses.

What if my adult child ages out of my plan coverage?

Once your child turns 26 and transitions off of your plan to his or her own plan, you and your child can begin or continue to contribute to your child's HSA if the child is still covered by an HDHP.

Your child can claim the HSA contributions you make to his or her account as an above-the-line income tax deduction (one taken when calculating adjusted gross income and available to taxpayers whether or not they itemize deductions).

What if I have more than one HSA?

If you have more than one HSA, your total yearly contributions to your HSAs combined cannot be more than the IRS-mandated limits of $3,450 for an individual in 2018 and $3,500 in 2019, or $6,900 for a family in 2018 and $7,000 in 2019, plus the $1,000 catch-up contribution for eligible individuals 55 and older.

What if my spouse also has an HDHP and an HSA?

If you and your spouse have self-only HDHPs under separate plans, you can each open an HSA and contribute the yearly maximum for an individual: $3,450 in 2018, and $3,500 in 2019.

If either spouse has family HDHP coverage and the other spouse does not have disqualifying coverage, you are both treated as having family HDHP coverage for annual contribution purposes.

If each spouse has an HSA and family coverage under a separate plan, the yearly HSA contribution limit for families is $6,900 in 2018 and $7,000 in 2019. You and your spouse can split the amount equally or in any way you want, provided your total contributions do not exceed the annual maximum (IRC Sec. 223(b)(5)(B)).

Each spouse 55 and older (and not enrolled in Medicare) can contribute an additional $1,000 catch-up contribution, whether enrolled in family or individual HDHPs, provided they each have an HSA.

What if I get divorced or become legally separated?

Spouses do not jointly own an HSA. Each must qualify to contribute to an HSA. In the event of a divorce or legal separation, the HSA owned by one spouse may be divided or given in part or full to the other spouse by court judgment.

Changing from family to single-only HDHP coverage

If you made the maximum family contribution to your HSA and kept your family coverage after the divorce or legal separation, you will not run into any issues with excess contributions.

However, if you and your spouse were covered by a family HSA-qualified HDHP and you change to single coverage after your divorce, you may need to adjust your contributions to ensure you do not over-contribute for the year. You may also want to talk to your tax preparer about how to deal with additional taxes and penalties due to possible excess contributions.

Determine if you made an excess contribution

You may have made an excess contribution if you get divorced and change your HDHP coverage to a single plan, have contributed more than $3,500 to your HSA during 2019, and you have not used the full-contribution rule—where the entire yearly contribution is made on the first day of the last month of the tax year. For more information, see chapter four. Excess contributions are considered income and subject to an additional six percent federal excise tax. Excess employer contributions are also subject to income tax and excise tax.

You may withdraw some or all of the excess contributions and not pay the excise tax— you are still liable for income tax on the amount— if you meet the following conditions:

- You withdraw the excess contributions by the due date of your tax return for the tax year during which the contributions were made.

- You withdraw any interest income earned on the withdrawn contributions and include the earnings as other income on your tax return for the tax year you withdraw the contributions and earnings (IRC Sec. 223(f)(3)). States may also have their own excise taxes.

Contributing the maximum family amount under the full-contribution rule

If you made a maximum yearly contribution for a family under the full-contribution rule, divorced mid-year, and changed your coverage to single under your health plan's HDHP, then you will have failed the testing period for eligibility under family coverage. You will have to include the excess contribution amount in your gross income for the current tax year and pay a 10 percent penalty on the amount.

Example

Making the maximum family contribution under the full-contribution rule, then changing to single coverage during the testing period

Janetta, age 41, enrolled with family coverage in her HDHP on October 1, 2018. Her husband, Jacob is a freelance cabinet maker and does not have his own insurance, so Janetta put him on her plan. They have no children.

Although she enrolled in her HDHP late in the plan year, she was HSA-eligible on December 1, 2018 and was eligible to make the 2018 maximum family contribution of $6,900 under the full-contribution rule.

Janetta and Jacob divorced in September 2019. In the divorce settlement, Janetta kept her HSA and changed to single-only coverage in her HDHP. Although she fulfilled the testing period by remaining in her HDHP, she did not fulfill the testing period for family coverage.

Janetta was still eligible for the maximum contribution for a single person under the full-contribution rule.

To determine her excess contribution for 2018, she subtracted the maximum contribution for single-only coverage ($3,450) from the $6,900 family contribution:

$6,900 - $3,450 = $3,450

On her 2018 tax return, Janetta added the excess $3,450 to her adjusted gross income and paid an additional 10 percent tax on that amount.

In January 2019, Janetta made a lump sum contribution of $7,000 thinking she would have family coverage all year. She wanted to have the money earn interest as quickly as possible.

Because she was still eligible for family coverage on September 1, 2019, she was eligible for nine months of family contributions.

She divided $7,000 and $3,500 by 12 to get the prorated monthly contribution for family and single-only coverage.

Family prorated monthly contribution: $7,000 / 12 = $583.33

Single-only prorated monthly contribution: $3,500 / 12 = $291.67

She multiplied the family monthly contribution by nine to get the amount of family-level contribution she was eligible for during 2019. Then she did the same for the single-level contribution for the three months after her divorce.

$583.33 x 9 = $5,249.98

$291.67 x 3 = $875.01

She added the two amounts to get her maximum allowable contribution for the year:

$5,249.98 + $875.01 = $6,124.99

Then she subtracted the amount from the $7,000 she had contributed to find out her excess contribution for 2018:

$7,000 - $6,124.99 = $875.01

Janetta added the $875.01 to her adjusted gross income on her 2019 return and paid the six percent excise tax for the excess contribution (the penalty was six percent instead of 10 percent because she did not make the overcontribution under the full-contribution rule).

COBRA coverage for the divorced spouse

(26 USC Sec. 4980B(f), and the regulations under 26 CFR Sec. 54.4980B-1 et seq)

If you and your spouse are both covered under a family plan through one of your employers and divorce, the spouse who is not employed by the plan's sponsor may be entitled to buy COBRA continuation coverage under the plan (for more information on COBRA, see US Department of Labor site, www.dol.gov/ebsa/faqs/faq-consumer-cobra.html).

Divorce is a qualifying COBRA event. Those eligible may be required to pay up to 102 percent of the employer's cost of coverage for COBRA, and they are entitled to coverage for a limited period of time (from 18 months to 36 months), depending on the qualifying event.

The eligibility period may, in some cases, be extended, if another qualifying event occurs during the period of COBRA eligibility.

What if I lose my job or my hours are reduced?

If you lose your job, change jobs, have your working hours reduced or your employer changes the plan it offers, you may no longer be covered by an HDHP. You may lose your eligibility to contribute to an HSA.

Losing your eligibility to contribute to an HSA does not mean you cannot use the HSA. You can still use any balance in the HSA for qualified medical expenses. You continue to own the account as is, even though you can no longer make contributions to it. If you become covered by a qualifying HDHP again in the future, you can resume contributions.

Using your HSA to pay COBRA premiums

(IRS Sec. 223(d)(2)(c)(1); IRS Notice 2004-2 Q&A 27, IRS Notice 2008-59 Q&A 32)

COBRA is an important safety net when you lose your employer-sponsored medical coverage. Although the premiums can appear expensive, COBRA coverage protects you in several ways:

- Your qualified medical expenses continue to be covered.

- You are credited for payments toward your deductible made during the current year.

- By maintaining continuous coverage under a health plan, you make it easier to get coverage for pre-existing conditions when you join another health plan later.

A number of job changes can trigger COBRA eligibility, including quitting your job, getting laid off, retiring or getting fired other than for gross misconduct (gross misconduct is not specifically defined in COBRA or in regulations under COBRA and depends on specific facts and circumstances). Generally, it is assumed that being fired for most ordinary reasons, such as excessive absences or generally poor performance, does not amount to gross misconduct.

If part-time employees are not covered under your plan, a reduction in hours can also trigger COBRA eligibility. A strike by unionized employees can qualify as a change in hours.

If you elect COBRA benefits, you can use your HSA to pay COBRA premiums and can continue to contribute to your HSA.

What if my spouse loses his or her own insurance coverage?

Having a baby is not the only reason you may need to change from self-only to family coverage.

If you have self-only coverage and your spouse loses coverage, you can change to family coverage without waiting for your open enrollment period if your employer allows. As in the case of a new child, your allowable HSA contribution also changes on the first day of the month during which your spouse becomes covered by the family HDHP.

What if I get a new job?

It is not uncommon for plans to impose a waiting period before newly hired employees can enroll. If you have a new job that imposes a waiting period and have either a self-only HSA-qualified HDHP or COBRA coverage from your last job, you can continue to make HSA contributions during this waiting period. You can also use your HSA funds to pay your COBRA premiums.

If your new employer does not have a waiting period

If your new employer has an HSA-qualified HDHP, look into rolling your old HSA over to the new one. You are allowed one rollover per year, though you can make an unlimited number of direct trustee-to-trustee transfers.

Know your state and local laws

COBRA is a federal law applicable to employers with at least 20 employees. Your state, county or city may also have a similar law that has broader coverage, covers even smaller firms or offers more generous coverage. If the state or local law is more generous than COBRA, the state or local law is the one that applies.

What if my employer's company closes or files for bankruptcy?

If your company closes or files for bankruptcy, then it may no longer have a health plan, and COBRA coverage will be unavailable.

If, however, another plan is offered through a successor employer, you may have COBRA rights through that employer. If you are offered COBRA coverage, you may use your HSA to pay those premiums.

If no COBRA coverage is available, you can use your HSA to pay for medical expenses or other coverage, including insurance premiums you might be able to buy while receiving unemployment compensation.

What if my plant or branch office is closed?

If your employer is subject to COBRA and your plant or branch office is closed but the rest of the company or a parent company remains in business, you must be offered COBRA coverage through your employer. You can use your HSA to pay those premiums.

What if my company is sold and I lose my job?

If your company is sold and you lose your job, the buyer may be obliged to provide you with COBRA coverage. If COBRA coverage is available, you can use your HSA to pay those premiums.

What if my employer drops my plan but stays in business?

Termination of a health plan does not trigger COBRA eligibility. You can no longer contribute to an HSA if your HDHP is terminated, but you can use your HSA for medical expenses. You can also opt for a traditional low-deductible health plan if offered by your employer. However, if you choose a traditional low-deductible health plan, you cannot contribute to your HSA.

What if I retire before I am eligible for Medicare?

Many people retire before age 65, the age for Medicare eligibility.

If you retire before age 65, you can use your HSA for a wide range of medical expenses. You can use it to pay COBRA premiums, premiums for long-term care insurance or non-COBRA premiums for coverage you may buy on your own (if you are receiving unemployment compensation). You may also use your HSA balance to directly pay for qualified medical expenses.

If you retire from your job, accept a pension from your employer and go to work for another employer, you cannot use your HSA to make premium payments your new employer may require, unless you are at least age 65.

What if I enroll in Medicare?

Once you enroll in Medicare, you are no longer eligible to make HSA contributions. Remember, enrolling in SSI (the income portion of Social Security) automatically enrolls you in Medicare Part A.

Like early retirees, you can use the HSA once you have reached age 65 to pay COBRA premiums, premiums for long-term care insurance or non-COBRA premiums for coverage you buy on your own (if you are receiving unemployment compensation). You can also use your HSA balance to pay qualified medical expenses directly.

If you remain employed after age 65, you can use your HSA to pay your share, if any, for employer-sponsored healthcare coverage.

If your employer offers healthcare coverage to retirees or their survivors and requires a premium contribution from participating retirees or survivors, your HSA can be used to pay for that coverage as well.

You can also use your HSA to pay Medicare premiums once you reach age 65.

Medicare recipients should realize that Medigap insurance—a private insurance that covers out-of-pocket costs not covered by Medicare—is not a qualified expense that can be paid with your HSA. Medigap is not the same thing as retiree health insurance; you buy a Medigap policy from a private insurer, while your employer provides retiree health insurance. If you have retiree health insurance, you will generally not need Medigap coverage (IRS Notice 2004-2 Q&A 27).

What if I declare bankruptcy or have other financial problems?

An HSA is not protected from creditors unless it qualifies as an employer-sponsored benefit plan under the Employee Retirement Income Security Act (ERISA) of 1974.

ERISA is the federal law that governs the terms under which private company employee benefit plans are offered. According to the U.S. Department of Labor, an HSA, whether offered by an employer or opened by an individual, is not necessarily an ERISA plan.

There is no exemption in the law specifically protecting HSA balances from the reach of bankruptcy creditors. This means that if the balance in the HSA is taken and used towards the outstanding debits of other creditors, the account holder is subject to income tax and the 20 percent penalty on the amount used for nonqualified withdrawals.

However, under the 2005 federal bankruptcy law, an individual debtor may deduct any reasonably necessary health insurance, disability insurance and health savings account expenses for the debtor, the spouse of the debtor or the dependents of the debtor when determining his or her statement of monthly income.

Can I use my HSA as collateral for a loan or cash it in to pay a debt? (IRC Sections 223(e)(2) and 4975, IRS Notice 2004-50 Q&A 67)

Account beneficiaries (the owner) and HSA trustees and custodians cannot enter into a prohibited transaction with the HSA. A prohibited transaction is the sale, exchange, or lease of property, borrowing or lending money, furnishing goods, services or facilities, transferring to or use by or for the benefit of the beneficiary of any assets contained in the account.

The beneficiary also may not pledge the assets of the HSA. Any amount used for such purposes is treated as a distribution and included in the beneficiary's gross income, because it is not used for medical expenses. A 20 percent excise tax penalty for such distributions applies (IRC Sec. 223(f)(4)(A)).

What if I become disabled?

Since you do not need to work in order to make HSA contributions, you can continue to be covered by your employer's or another HSA-qualified HDHP plan after becoming disabled.

If you are covered by an HSA-qualified HDHP and qualify for short-term or long-term disability benefits under your employer-sponsored plan, nothing should change if your employer's healthcare coverage remains the same during the disability period.

However, there are important cautions. Your HSA has to be paired with an HDHP, so if you lose HDHP coverage under your employer's plan because you can no longer work, you will no longer be eligible to contribute to an HSA unless you qualify for COBRA or can find a qualifying HDHP as an individual. You can use your HSA balance to make COBRA payments if you become eligible for COBRA coverage.

Note: If you must take a distribution from your HSA for non-medical expenses because you are disabled, the distribution will be subject to income tax but not to excise tax (IRC Sec. 223(f)(4)(B)).

HSAs and social security disability insurance

If you qualify for Social Security Disability Insurance (SSDI) benefits, everything changes. Qualifying for SSDI benefits is a separate process from qualifying for benefits under an employer-sponsored disability plan. By law, to qualify for SSDI benefits, you must be unable to do any substantial amount of work* due to your health, your condition must have lasted a year and be expected to last at least a year, or be expected to result in your death.

Applicants have to be unable to do substantial work for at least five months before filing an application. Roughly half of SSDI applications are rejected. If you are awarded SSDI benefits, you become eligible for Medicare coverage two years later. Once you are covered by Medicare, you are no longer eligible to make HSA contributions.

You can use your HSA both during the application process and after you are awarded benefits. Prior to being awarded SSDI benefits, you can use your HSA to pay COBRA premiums if eligible (IRC Sec. 223(d)(2)(c)(1). You can also use your HSA for other medical expenses.

*According to IRS Publication 524, "Substantial gainful activity is the performance of significant duties over a reasonable period of time while working for pay or profit, or in work generally done for pay or profit. Full-time work (or part-time work done at your employer's convenience) in a competitive work situation for at least the minimum wage conclusively shows that you're able to engage in substantial gainful activity".

What if I die?

When the account owner dies, any amount remaining in the HSA passes to the entity or individual named as the HSA's beneficiaries. If the owner's surviving spouse is the named beneficiary, the HSA becomes the HSA of the surviving spouse (IRC Sec. 223(f)(8)(A); IRS Notice 2004-2 Q&A 31).

An HSA is considered an individual account, and as such, the spouse inheriting the HSA is considered the owner. The spouse can then use the HSA as any other HSA owner would. The surviving spouse is subject to income tax on amounts in the account only if not used for qualified medical expenses.

If the HSA passes to a person or persons other than a surviving spouse, then the HSA ceases to be an HSA, and the heir or heirs are required to include the fair market value of the HSA as gross income (IRC Sec. 223(f)(8)(B)(i)). Fair market value is calculated as of the date of the account owner's death and is reduced by any payments made from the HSA on behalf of the decedent within one year of death (IRC Sec. 223(f)(8)(B)(ii)).

Choose a beneficiary when you set up your HSA. What happens to your HSA when you die depends on who you designate as the beneficiary. If your estate is the beneficiary, the value of your HSA is included on your final income tax return.

Things to remember

- Research all options for using your HSA. Familiarize yourself with qualified medical expenses, investment options and other rules and regulations.

- Qualifying life events—marriage, divorce, new baby, stepchildren, adoption, changing or losing a job, disability, death—all present new coverage needs. Be sure to make the necessary enrollment changes as soon as the opportunity presents itself.

- In most cases, you must make your enrollment or coverage changes within 30 days of the life event.

- HSAs can help you with employment changes and transitions in and out of the workforce.

- Enrolling in Medicare puts an end to making contributions to your HSA. However, you can still use the funds you have built up in your HSA for a variety of expenses.

- Update your HSA beneficiary to avoid confusion and unnecessary taxes for your heirs when you die.

CHAPTER 8
Using an HSA with other tax-advantaged accounts

For more than a decade, employers have offered other types of consumer-directed health plans (CDHPs) such as health reimbursement arrangements (HRAs), flexible spending accounts (FSAs), and state and federal archer medical spending accounts (MSAs). These accounts are used to pay for medical co-payments, dependent care, dental and vision expenses, and other costs with tax-deductible or pre-tax dollars.

Each kind of account offers its own unique advantages. In some situations, supplementing HSAs with different combinations of special-purpose FSAs or HRAs gives an employer useful options for making a CDHP strategy better fit both their needs and the needs of their employees.

FSAs and HRAs can also be effective ways to stretch your HSA balance and maximize money you save or use.

You remain eligible to contribute to an HSA if you have a limited-purpose FSA or HRA, as opposed to traditional general-purpose versions of these accounts.

Post-deductible FSAs and HRAs can also be used with an HSA.

Background

MSAs and Archer MSAs

MSAs and Archer MSAs have existed since the mid-1990s. This federal pilot program was limited to small employers and the self-employed as an affordable alternative to high-priced, low-deductible health plans. MSAs required the individual to also have an HDHP. Savings in the MSA could be rolled over year to year.

MSAs were superseded by HSAs, and existing MSAs grandfathered. The pilot program for Archer MSAs ended December 31, 2007, and no new Archer MSAs can be opened.

HRAs

HRAs are benefit plans that employers can fund and offer as a standalone or with other health benefits. Employers have complete flexibility to customize their HRA plan design. Unused funds may rollover to a subsequent HRA plan year, depending on the plan design.

In an HRA, the employer offers an account from which the employee is reimbursed for qualified medical expenses, such as co-payments, deductibles, vision care, prescriptions and dental expenses. Reimbursements are tax-free for the employee and tax-deductible for the employer. Self-employed persons are not eligible to participate in an HRA.

FSAs*

An FSA allows employees to set aside pre-tax earnings to pay for benefits or expenses that are not covered by insurance or other benefit plans, such as co-pays, deductibles, dental and vision expenses.

The law allows employers to rollover $500 in their employees' FSAs to the following year. Employers must choose between offering employees the option to rollover their FSA dollars to the next year, or to have a grace period option for claims incurred after the end of the year. The choice must be documented in the plan, and applies to all employees. The employer cannot select rollover for some employees and grace period for others (IRS Notice 2013-71).

*In this book, we use FSA to mean a healthcare FSA. There is also dependent care FSA which is not relevant to this book.

Check with your employer to find out which FSA option they offer.

If you are enrolled in a general healthcare FSA with a grace period and you decide to enroll in an HSA-qualified plan for the following year, you will not be able to contribute to an HSA until your run-out period ends and you have no funds remaining in your general healthcare FSA.

If you are enrolled in a general healthcare FSA with a rollover feature, the unused funds in an FSA will rollover to the following plan year even if you do not make an election for that year. You will not be able to contribute to an HSA if you are covered by an FSA with amounts that rolled over.

Using HSAs with other benefit plan options

The IRS allows employers to offer HRAs and FSAs with an HSA. HSAs can also be used with employee assistance plans (EAPs) and cafeteria plans.

Having general healthcare FSAs and HRAs can make you ineligible to contribute to an HSA. However, employers are allowed to offer restricted FSAs and HRAs along with their HSA-qualified HDHPs, as long as the FSAs and HRAs meet certain requirements.

Limited-purpose FSA (LPFSA) or limited-purpose HRA (Rev. Rul. 2004-45)

One way for employers to offer an FSA or HRA to employees covered by an HSA-qualified HDHP is to offer a limited-purpose version of these plans.

A limited-purpose FSA (LPFSA) or a limited-purpose HRA (LPHRA) may be restricted to paying for permitted coverage benefits, such as only dental and vision expenses. Limited-purpose FSAs and HRAs work in parallel with an HSA; both kinds of accounts may be used to pay for expenses at the same time. One advantage of an LPFSA is that all of the money in the account is available to you at the start of the plan year, even if you have not made all of your contributions to the account.

It makes sense to contribute to an LPFSA if you choose to contribute the entire allowable yearly maximum to your HSA. The main disadvantage is that you must forfeit all unspent FSA funds at year-end or when the run-out or grace periods ends, unless your employer allows you to rollover up to $500.

Example

Maximizing tax-advantages through an LPFSA

Spencer has an HSA with an LPFSA that covers vision and dental expenses only.

Last year when his wife, Melissa, took their young son to the dentist, they were advised he would need a dental appliance to correct a jaw problem. Melissa asked the dentist for a cost estimate. She also got an estimate for dental work Spencer would need during the coming year.

Melissa also wants to replace her prescription sunglasses. She contacts several optical shops to compare costs and gets estimates for exams, frames, and lenses.

In 2019, Spencer and Melissa want to maximize their HSA, so they can start investing it. Spencer sets up his payroll deductions to contribute the full maximum for a family—$7,000. Then he elects to contribute $2,300 to his FSA (based on the estimates for dental work and glasses).

This equals $9,300 in income Spencer and Melissa are able to protect from taxes.

With the FSA to pay the dental and vision expenses, Spencer and Melissa are able to invest their entire HSA contribution for the year in a mutual fund.

Post-deductible healthcare FSA or HRA (Rev. Rul. 2004-45)

Alternatively, a general-purpose healthcare FSA or an HRA can be set up to provide benefits only after the minimum annual deductible specified in the HDHP has been satisfied. This is called a post-deductible FSA or post-deductible HRA.

In this case, the FSA or HRA works in cooperation with the HSA. These arrangements cannot pay or reimburse any medical expenses incurred before the IRS minimum annual deductible amount is met. After that, the account can cover any remaining co-payments or coinsurance for which you are responsible.

If your employer provides an HSA-qualified HDHP with a post-deductible FSA or HRA, you can submit your receipts for reimbursement only after you meet your IRS minimum deductible.

Example

Covering the gap between the deductible and the HDHP's out-of-pocket maximum

Kelly's employer offers an HDHP with a $3,000 deductible and a $4,000 out-of-pocket maximum.

To help close the gap between the plan's deductible and the out-of-pocket maximum, Kelly's employer also offers a $500 post-deductible HRA.

Kelly has a lot of medical expenses during the year and she spends her entire HSA contribution of $3,500. After meeting her deductible and paying her coinsurance, she submits a reimbursement request to her employer and receives $500 from the HRA.

Combining two kinds of FSAs and HRAs (Rev. Rul. 2004-45)

An FSA and HRA can each be a combination of both limited-purpose and post-deductible, as long as the employer has it written accordingly in the plan document.

Suspended HRA

Before the beginning of an HRA coverage period, you can elect to suspend an HRA. The HRA does not pay or reimburse the medical expenses incurred during the suspension period, except for preventive care and items listed under other health coverage. When the suspension period ends, you are no longer eligible to make contributions to an HSA.

Retirement HRA

A retirement HRA pays or reimburses only those medical expenses incurred after retirement (and no expenses incurred before retirement). In this case, the individual is an eligible individual for the purpose of making contributions to the HSA before retirement, but they lose eligibility for coverage periods when the retirement HRA begins to pay or reimburse section 213(d) medical expenses. Therefore, after retirement, the individual can no longer contribute to an HSA.

Employee assistance programs (EAPs)
(IRS Notice 2004-50 Q&A 10)

An EAP is an employee benefit that covers all or part of the cost for employees to receive counseling, referrals and advice in dealing with stressful issues in their lives.

An employee covered by an EAP, wellness program or a disease management plan can still contribute to an HSA—as long as these plans do not provide substantial medical benefits.

Cafeteria plans

An employer may offer an HSA as part of a cafeteria plan, an employee benefit plan that allows employees to choose benefits from a number of different options, including 401(k), health insurance, other insurance and time off. HSA contributions can be made through cafeteria plans (IRC Sec. 125(d)(2)(D); Prop. Treas. Reg. 1.125-1(a)(3)(j)(2007)).

Many of the rules governing HSAs offered as part of a cafeteria plan are different from those governing HSAs offered outside of such a plan. For example, an employer offering an HSA as part of a cafeteria plan can structure its contributions as matching contributions, which means the employee receives an employer contribution only if the employee also contributes to the account. In such a situation, some employees might not receive any contributions to an HSA or might receive contributions that differ in dollar amounts or as a percentage of the HDHP deductible.

In contrast, an employer offering an HSA that is not part of a cafeteria plan must ensure that all eligible participating employees receive a comparable contribution to their HSA plan—either in dollar terms or as a percentage of the HDHP deductible (IRC Sec. 4980G, Treas. Reg. Sec. 54.4980G-5 Q&A 1 and 2).

At the same time, employer HSA contributions made under a cafeteria plan must meet nondiscrimination rules applicable to cafeteria plans. These are the same rules applied for 401(k)s and FSAs, to ensure that a plan does not favor the employer's most highly compensated employees (Treas. Reg. Sec. 54.4980G-5 Q&A 1, IRC Sec. 125(b), (c) and (g)).

Paying for a medical expense covered by more than one account

You cannot be reimbursed for the same medical expense from more than one account or arrangement. If you have an HSA, a healthcare FSA, and/or an HRA that pay or reimburse the same medical expense, you can select which account you would like to use to reimburse yourself. You can even divide the reimbursable amount between accounts if the balance of one account is not sufficient to cover the entire expense. However, you must maintain records to show that the distributions were used exclusively to pay or reimburse qualified medical expenses, that the qualified medical expenses have not been previously paid or reimbursed from another source and that the medical expenses have not been taken as an itemized deduction in any prior taxable year.*

*Subject to the rules in IRS Notice 2004-50.

Contributing to an HSA during the FSA grace period

General-purpose FSA grace period

(Prop. Treas. Reg. Sec. 1.125-1(e)(2007), IRS Notices 2005-42, 2007-22, and 2005-86, modified by IRC Sec. 223(c)(1)(B)(iii))

If you have a general-purpose healthcare FSA, it may provide you with a grace period of up to two-and-a-half months after the plan year ends—a total of 14½ months—to use balances accumulated in your account during the plan year. Most grace periods let you continue to incur expenses and get reimbursed, while a run-out period lets you only be reimbursed for expenses incurred during the plan year. A grace period is not automatic; your employer must draft the plan document to include this feature.

You are eligible to make HSA contributions during an FSA grace period that spills into the next plan year if the balance in the general-purpose healthcare FSA at the end of the prior plan year is zero (IRC Sec. 223(c)(1)(B)(iii)).

If you still have funds in the general-purpose FSA during the grace period, you cannot begin contributing to your HSA for the current plan year until the first day of the month following the end of the grace period.

Examples

General-purpose healthcare FSA with a balance carried into the grace period

Vernon ended his traditional plan, general healthcare FSA coverage on December 31, 2018, and he began an HSA-qualified HDHP on January 1, 2019. Because he still has money in the FSA at the beginning of the new plan year, he cannot begin contributing to his new HSA until after the FSA's grace period ends on March 15, 2019. Because HSA eligibility always begins on the first day of the month, he must wait until April 1, 2019, to make his first HSA contribution.

General-purpose healthcare FSA with a zero balance

Anita had a traditional health plan and a general healthcare FSA in 2018. She starts her HDHP and HSA on January 1, 2019. She is still technically covered by her FSA during the grace period until March 15, 2019. However, because she had spent her FSA down to zero by December 31, 2018, she can begin contributing to her HSA on January 1, 2019.

LPFSA grace period

You do not lose your eligibility to contribute to an HSA if you have funds in an LPFSA during the FSA grace period.

Example

LPFSA with a balance carried into the grace period

Lorenzo had an LPFSA that only covered vision and dental during 2018. On January 1, 2019, he begins his new HSA-qualified HDHP coverage.

Although there are still funds in the FSA during the FSA's grace period in the new plan year, there is nothing to stop him from making contributions to his HSA starting on January 1, 2019. Because his FSA is limited-purpose, it does not make Lorenzo ineligible to contribute to his HSA.

CHAPTER 9
Taxes, paperwork and recordkeeping

Why recordkeeping is important

The balance in your HSA is your money. Treat it and related records as you would your retirement plan, any other savings account or a credit card. Make sure you understand the charges to your account and get explanations for any you do not understand or do not belong to you.

Disputes or questions about billing and payments can arise even a year or two after a procedure or office visit. To reduce these issues, it is particularly important to keep records that allow you to reconstruct how you have spent your money.

It is also important to have records to back up deductions claimed on your tax return, in case you are audited by the IRS.

Submitting expenses

Keeping track of HSA expenses, contributions and earnings is much like sorting expenses you deduct on your income taxes from those you cannot deduct. You have to learn a new paradigm for sorting health expenses by category.

Submitting expenses to the HDHP

If your provider participates in your plan's network, the provider should submit your claim to your insurance plan. If not, you may have to file the claim yourself, so your expense is credited toward your deductible, out-of-pocket limit or both. The plan should supply you with a form for filing claims, but many providers give you enough information on your walk-out statement—what you get as you leave the office—that you can use the statement itself to file your claim. Keep copies of your statement in case of a dispute.

Requesting distributions from the HSA

You can pay HSA-eligible expenses with a debit card if one is provided by your HSA administrator, or with a checkbook that draws from your HSA. Alternatively, you can pay using your own account or credit card and submit the expense for reimbursement.

Some HSA administrators let account holders electronically transfer funds from the HSA to their own account for reimbursement.

Regardless of how you get reimbursed, you can only be reimbursed for the expenses you incurred after your HSA was established (IRS Notice 2004-50 Q&A 39).

Unlike an HDHP or an FSA, your trustee or custodian is not required to determine whether the distributions are for qualified medical expenses. It is up to you to maintain the proper records. They may limit the use of the debit card at certain merchants, but it is still your responsibility to keep accurate records.

Submitting expenses to an FSA

If you had an FSA in the past and your employer converts to an HDHP with a limited purpose FSA (LPFSA), then you will not have a lot of new processes or paperwork to learn. You submitted expenses to your old FSA by providing an EOB or itemized receipt; an LPFSA is likely to work the same way.

Paperwork you will receive

Invoices and point-of-sale receipts

Even though most over-the-counter medications required a doctor's prescription in order to be considered a medical expense as of January 1, 2011 per the health reform law, there are still many other items you can purchase with your HSA through retail stores such as diabetic supplies, canes, reading glasses and bandages (see appendix C).

The important thing to remember is to be sure all receipts and invoices have as much detail about the goods or services provided or purchased as possible, including date, item, service description, vendor, etc.

Explanation of benefits (EOB)

The EOB is a summary of charges and payment responsibilities provided by your health plan. It shows how much your health plan paid the provider, how much the provider originally charged, and the contracted discounts to which your providers have agreed.

The EOB also shows your financial responsibility. The EOB summarizes the cost of the services provided during the doctor's visit and updates the owner's progress toward meeting the plan deductible.

Note that the EOB also explains the participant's right to dispute any statements made in the EOB.

HSA statement

Your HSA administrator should send or make available a periodic statement containing the following details concerning your account: contributions you or your employer may have made on your behalf, payments made to providers from your HSA, investment and interest earnings accrued to your account, and fees your account may have incurred. Keep your statements the same way you do for other financial accounts—possibly in the same place.

Sample of explanation of benefits

THIS IS NOT A BILL
(Please keep this form for your records)

EXPLANATION OF BENEFITS (EOB)

John Doe
123 Any Street
Any Town, ST, 90062

Date: **March 12, 2019**
Benefit plan number: **XYZ00000000A**
Page number: **1 of 1**

Participant: **John Doe**
Patient: **John Doe**
Relationship: **Subscriber**

Member services
Local: **000.000.0000**
National: **800.000.0000**

Payment Summary						
Patient/claim no.	Paid to	Total charges	Covered amount	Previously processed	Patient responsibility
John D 1234567890		$135.00	$60.00	$0.00	$75.00

Subscriber's responsibility: **$75.00**
Does not reflect any payments you may have made to the provider.

Year-to-date cost sharing status: 2019

Applied to $3,000 per member deductible:
John D.   **$75.00**
$75.00 has accumulated toward deductible maximum.

Sample of periodic HSA statement

John Doe
123 Any Street
Any Town, ST, 90062

If you have any questions, please call 800.000.0000

Account statement
Account number: **123456**
Period: **06/01/2018 to 06/30/2019**
Statement print date: **07/01/2019**

Date	Description of transaction	Deposit (or withdrawal)	Account balance
		Beginning balance	$ 8,803.98
06/02/2019	Employer contribution (Tax year: 2019)	$83.33	$8,887.31
06/02/2019	Employee contribution (Tax year: 2019)	$89.58	$8,976.89
06/03/2019	Payment for claim 219325-0142	($15.00)	$8,961.89
06/15/2019	Employee contribution (Tax year: 2019)	$89.58	$9,051.47
06/15/2019	Employer contribution (Tax year: 2019)	$249.99	$9,301.46
06/21/2019	Payment for claim 219325-0143	($102.74)	$9,198.72
06/30/2019	Payment for claim 219325-0146	($244.69)	$8,954.03
06/30/2019	Investment: Fund A	($1,043.10)	$7,910.93
06/30/2019	Investment: Fund B	($695.40)	$7,215.53
06/30/2019	Investment: Fund C	($1,043.13)	$6,172.40
06/30/2019	Investment: Fund D	($695.40)	$5,477.00
06/30/2019	Investment: Fund E	($695.40)	$4,781.60
06/30/2019	Investment: Fund F	($695.40)	$4,086.20
06/30/2019	Investment: Fund G	($695.40)	$3,390.80
06/30/2019	Investment: Fund H	($695.40)	$2,695.40
06/30/2019	Investment: Fund I	($695.40)	$2,000.00
06/30/2019	Interest for Jun-19 (Annual percentage yield earned for period is 1.25% on average collected balance of $8,864.03)	$9.18	$2,009.18
		Ending balance	$ 2,009.18

Investment portfolio

Fund	Category	Shares	Closing price	Closing value
Fund A	Small Cap Fund	73.14	$18.71	$1,368.45
Fund B	Small Cap Stock Index	82.71	$16.34	$1,351.48
Fund C	Blue Chip Value	223.25	$9.10	$2,031.58
Fund D	Emerging Markets	34.82	$41.06	$1,429.71
Fund E	International Market Masters	93.76	$15.12	$1,417.65
Fund F	Appreciation Fund	43.90	$31.39	$1,378.02
Fund G	Capital Appreciation	66.34	$20.72	$1,374.56
Fund H	Equity Income Fund	69.49	$19.52	$1,356.44
Fund I	Large Cap Index	108.47	$18.89	$2,049.00
			Ending balance	$13,756.89

You can spend your HSA over a considerable amount of time

Because an HSA can also function as a long-term savings vehicle, you can accumulate funds over a considerable period of time. There is no time limit for claiming a reimbursement from your account, as long as you incur the expense you are claiming after the HSA was established. That may mean you need to produce or recover records about contributions to the account long after a transaction occurred (for example, what was paid out of the account, and when and why the transaction was made).

A provider who is slow to bill can complicate your life

Some busy hospitals or medical practices can lose your claim or bill. There have been cases where the doctor's office filed the claim online and it came through illegibly, so the office filed it again and it came through illegibly again. Or maybe the hospital or doctor's office changed billing systems and some claims were lost in the transition. End result: The bill goes unsubmitted for payment for many months.

Any plan is responsible for covered expenses you incur while a member of that plan, but once the plan is closed, their responsibility expires.

Your former plan has to keep a reserve so claims participants can submit expenses after the plan is closed. However, this reserve may not be very large and can get exhausted before a late claim is considered.

That is not necessarily the slow-billing provider's problem. When you went in for your visit or procedure, you signed papers saying you would pay if your plan did not.

Always alert providers if you are changing insurance plans or have been advised that your employer is planning to do so. Encourage providers to submit any outstanding bills promptly.

Keeping track of deductibles

The EOB you receive from your HDHP will show your progress toward meeting the plan limits for the year. Make sure you know how to interpret the deductible information in the EOB and always try to work from the most recent statement so you can make the right decisions about your care and how to pay for it.

Different rules may apply to in-network and out-of-network care

Most plans that include provider networks apply different out-of-pocket limits, deductibles, or both, to in-network and out-of-network care. In a traditional plan, this did not matter to you, unless you or your family had a particularly costly year.

In an HSA-qualified HDHP, your deductible may be half or more of your out-of-pocket limit, so you are more likely to hit the out-of-pocket limit than in a traditional plan. This means you may want to keep track of your in-network and out-of-network spending and adjust your provider choices if you are close to meeting one limit but not the other.

Example

Selecting a network provider

Suppose Roy has a self-only plan with a $1,700 out-of-pocket limit for in-network care and a $2,600 limit for out-of-network care.

In-network care is insured at 100 percent; out-of-network care at 80 percent. His plan's deductible is $1,700.

Roy has spent $1,600 so far this year for in-network care and $250 for out-of-network care. He is considering foot surgery that will cost $2,000.

He can choose an in-network provider or one out of his network. If he chooses an in-network provider, he will pay $100, no matter what price the provider has negotiated with his plan. If he chooses an out-of-network provider, he will pay $400 ($2,000 x 20 percent non-network coinsurance).

If you are not in an integrated plan

If you do not have an HSA administrator that integrates with your insurance company and gives you a history of all of the claims paid by your HSA, be especially diligent about tracking your payments.

Always reconcile the paperwork you receive from your HDHP with statements from your HSA. If you have had a problem with your HDHP or HSA, you may have to follow up with both your health plan and HSA administrator to make sure errors are corrected in both accounts.

Disputing charges

If you get a bill that does not make sense, call your provider's office, the customer service number provided for your plan or both. If someone sent you an incorrect statement, it can become a problem later, unless you do something about it.

Everybody makes mistakes and a busy medical practice, in particular, will be dealing with a large number of plans that may be constantly changing requirements and patients whose plans are changing as well. Keep track and follow up.

When you disagree with your HDHP

Some of the same claims-processing errors possible under a standard insurance plan can also happen under an HSA-qualified HDHP. An in-network provider's invoice might be incorrectly processed as out-of-network, or the birth date for a participant could be incorrectly recorded, resulting in a denial of benefits.

Because your progress toward meeting the year's deductible can be affected, it is recommended that you immediately follow up on any errors.

When you disagree with your HSA statement

If you have never had an unauthorized charge appear on a credit card, you are part of an elite club. You do not have to be a victim of identity theft—a simple processing error can put a charge on your account that belongs to someone else.

If your HSA custodian issues you a debit or credit-type card, review charges on your HSA just as you do the charges on your credit card statements.

Understand your rights to have a disputed charge investigated, removed or both. If your HSA issues your checks, understand your rights to stop payment on a check, and what to do if you lose your checkbook. The laws governing checkbooks and debit cards are not the same. Therefore, your rights to dispute a claim will vary depending on how the account was used.

You are responsible for documenting how you used your HSA

In a traditional plan, your plan pays for only what it covers. Typically, the covered services are outlined in the plan documents you get from your insurer or the summary plan description (SPD) you get from your employer.

The HSA, in contrast, can be used for a wide range of expenses limited only by HSA legislation and generally what is accepted by the IRS for itemized medical deductions.

You need to understand what the allowable uses are and back up your claims with receipts. If you do not, you may face a 20 percent penalty plus taxes for unauthorized distributions. If you spend the money on items other than eligible medical expenses, you will also be required to pay income taxes on those expenses.

Keep your original documents

Any home financial software or spreadsheet program can be used to help you budget and keep track of medical expenses. However, if you need to substantiate or contest a claim, you will need the original documents. Some HSA administrators provide mobile apps to conveniently photograph and store these documents.

Keeping good records helps avoid confusion

Your HSA can pay for certain expenses that are not covered by your HDHP. For example, your HSA can be used for chiropractic services that might not be covered by your HDHP benefits.

Keep your HSA records as long as the account remains open, even if you have moved your account to a different bank or other company from the one where you first established your account and you are no longer eligible to contribute to your account.

The importance of the calendar

There are several reasons it is important to keep track of when expenses occurred and when they were paid.

Coordinating account management with the IRS calendar

The HSA is a tax-favored account, so the IRS determines how you can spend your balance. You can wait as long as you want after an expense has been incurred to submit it to your HSA (find more information later in this chapter on how long to keep HSA records). However, no matter how old the expense is, you must be prepared to fully document it in the year you claim it.

Coordinating account management with the HDHP calendar

Your employer may change from an HDHP offered by one company to one offered by another, or may eliminate your HDHP entirely and move to another plan design.

If you change HDHPs, be sure any expenses you accrue are paid by the correct plan and coordinate your HSA with the new HDHP. If your employer changes plans and you are no longer covered by an HDHP, then you need to keep track of when this happens, as you will not be able to contribute to your HSA as of the first day of the first month after the month your HDHP coverage ends. For example, if your HDHP coverage ends on June 15, you are no longer eligible to contribute to your HSA as of July 1. However, you can continue to use the funds in your HSA for eligible expenses.

How long to keep receipts, statements and other documentation

You are responsible for documenting that your HSA distributions were made for qualified purposes. The HSA custodian or trustee, your insurer and your employer are responsible for various aspects of your account reporting, but not this.

The IRS can generally audit most individual taxpayers for three years after the extended due date of the return (IRC Sec. 6501(a)). This means if your income tax return for 2018 is due April 15, 2019 but you file for the automatic extension to August 15, the IRS can audit you until August 15, 2022.

In some situations, the audit period can be six years instead of three (for example, if you understate an item of income that is 25 percent or more than the total you have reported). Neither of these limitations applies if tax fraud or tax evasion is involved (IRC Sec. 6501(e)(1)(A) (6 year rule), 6501(c) (fraud rule)).

It is suggested that you keep records documenting your HSA distributions for at least the period of time your income tax return is considered open, or subject to audit, and preferably for as long as you maintain the account.

Avoiding "the shoebox effect"

Even if your HSA provider gives you a debit card, credit card or a checkbook, you may end up submitting claims yourself because you forgot to use the HSA, or because you may not have had enough money at the time of the expense to pay claims.

If you place your receipts in a shoebox intending to get to them later, you may miss out on important benefits from your account and you may end up using post-tax dollars when HSA funds were available.

Establish a clearly labeled file and keep track of what you have already submitted, what has been paid and what is still outstanding. If your health plan offers online access to EOBs, get in the habit of using your plan website as a ready-made filing system.

HSA and HDHP records made easy

A simple system for keeping track of your HSA and HDHP records

Use a simple multipocket folder available in any stationery supply store, a three-ring binder with separators, or scan documents. Financial reports provided by your HSA administrator or by household budget programs, such as Quicken, can also help you track your expenses. Original documents or photocopies of receipts will be required in the event of an IRS audit. After you have picked your organization system, set up the following sections:

- **Bills and proofs of payment for care obtained from in-network providers.** Include canceled checks or credit card receipts for any bills you did not pay directly from your HSA.

- **Bills and proofs of payment for care obtained from out-of-network providers.** Again, include canceled checks or credit card receipts for any bills you did not pay directly from your HSA.

- **EOBs from network providers, arranged in reverse chronological order (most recent on top), so you can easily track your progress toward meeting HDHP limits that may apply to your network care.**

- **EOBs from out-of-network providers, again arranged in reverse chronological order, so you can easily track your progress toward meeting any separate HDHP limits that may apply to out-of-network care.** You may not need separate files for in-network and out-of-network care if your HDHP does not apply separate limits.

- **Bills and proofs of payment for healthcare spending that are not covered under your plan, and therefore are not counted toward your deductible.** Such spending could include the excess cost of braille reading material for a blind person or transportation costs to see a specialist in another city.

- **Periodic statements from your HSA trustee or custodian.** For ease of reference, you may want to arrange this part of your file in reverse chronological order as well so the first statement you see is the most current.

Label your file with the current year and set up a new file every year. This will make it easier to track bills and reimbursements as time passes.

Eligibility for tax deductions

The employer, employee, or individual, depending on who makes the contribution, may claim deductions for HSA contributions. HSAs qualify as a deduction for federal and most state taxes.

Deducting contributions from others

Although parties other than the account holder or their employer can make contributions to the account holder's HSA, those third parties cannot deduct the contribution from their taxes.

However, the account holder who received the contribution can deduct the contribution from his or her gross income.

Example

Contributing to an adult child's HSA

Ernesto and Maria's son Carlos is 25 and attending college. Carlos is too old to qualify as a tax dependent, but young enough to be covered by his father's HDHP.

Ernesto helps Carlos open his own HSA and makes a $1,000 contribution to the HSA.

Ernesto and Maria cannot deduct the $1,000 on their own tax return, but Carlos can exclude it from gross income on his.

Storing records electronically

If you choose to store your records electronically, we suggest you have both on-site and off-site back ups (in case of disaster, you computer and on-site backup can both be damaged). If you plan on storing your back up 'in the cloud' using services like Microsoft® OneDrive, Google® Drive, or DropBox®, note that these storages may not be encrypted, meaning hackers or the government can see the contents you store there.

Income tax deductions for the employee or individual purchaser

The tax-deductible contribution amount is calculated on a month-to-month basis, based on the total amount of the deduction and the number of months of participation.

The contribution is an above-the-line deduction for the purpose of calculating adjusted gross income, unless done through a cafeteria plan.

Example

Choosing to use the HSA contribution as an above-the-line deduction

Hank, a single taxpayer, makes $36,000 a year and contributes $1,000 to his HSA.

On his tax return, he can only deduct medical expenses that exceed 7.5 percent of his adjusted gross income if he itemizes his deductions on Schedule A.

Hank has not had any medical expenses for the year. He decides that it is better to take an above-the-line deduction by subtracting the $1,000 HSA contribution when calculating his adjusted gross income.

Double-dipping is not allowed

You cannot count an HSA contribution twice by calculating it against your gross income and then deducting it as an itemized medical expense. In fact, no expense can be deducted twice or paid twice from different tax-exempt accounts or through different insurance plans.

However, as an eligible individual you can deduct a contribution on your tax return even if another person makes it on your behalf (IRS Notice 2004-2 Q&A 18).

Employer-provided coverage (IRS Notice 2004-2 Q&A 19)

Contributions an employer makes to the employee's HSA are treated as employer-provided coverage for medical expenses under an accident or health plan and are excludable from the employee's gross income if made on behalf of an eligible individual.

Employer contributions are not subject to income tax withholding from wages or to the Federal Insurance Contributions Act (FICA), the Federal Unemployment Tax Act (FUTA), or the Railroad Retirement Tax Act.

Employer contributions may be subject to certain state taxes.

Contributions for the self-employed and owners of S corporations

Self-employed individuals and greater than two percent owners of S corporations are not considered employees. As such, they cannot receive employer contributions. However, they can make their own contributions and claim the above-the-line deduction on their personal income tax return.

Contributions to the HSA made by a bona fide partner are treated as a distributive share of partnership income, and they are considered guaranteed payments derived from the partnership's trade or business and reported as such on IRS Schedule–K1 (Form 1065). The contributions are included in the partner's net earnings from which the partner is then able to deduct those contributions as an adjustment to gross income, just as any HSA owner is able to do within the confines of the law.

Contributions to the HSA of a greater than two percent shareholder-employee in consideration for services rendered are treated as a guaranteed payment, and are includable in the greater than two percent shareholder-employee's net earnings. The contributions can then be deducted as an adjustment to gross income.

Tax deductions for the employer

To be tax-deductible, employer HSA contributions must be comparable for all employees. There is one exception to this rule. Employers may contribute more to HSAs for non-highly compensated employees (IRC Sec. 4980G(e), Treas. Reg. Sec. 54.4980G-6). The IRS uses the same definition of highly compensated employees for HSAs as they do for other retirement accounts.

Contributions are considered comparable if the employer makes the same contributions on behalf of all eligible participating employees with comparable coverage during the same period. Contributions are considered comparable if they are either the same dollar amount or the same percentage of the deductible under the HDHP (Treas. Reg. Sec. 54.4980G-4).

For example, Company A's contribution is considered comparable for all employees if each eligible employee gets $500 toward an HSA. Company B's contribution is also considered comparable for all employees if it covers 75 percent of the deductible.

Even when a husband and wife work for the same employer, the HSAs and contributions made to the accounts must be separate. Otherwise, comparability rules may be breached because it could be seen that one individual was receiving twice the contribution rather than half of a joint contribution (Treas. Reg. Sec. 54.4980G-3 Q&A 8).

Except under cafeteria plans, an employer may not institute matching contributions to HSAs (Treas. Reg. Sec. 54.4980G-4 Q&A 8). Comparability rules do not apply when contributions are made through cafeteria plans, however, discrimination testing rules do apply.

IRS-compliant paperwork

Form W-2

Wage and tax statement

Employers must generally file a W-2 Form for any employee that was paid wages for a given year. Employees must enclose a copy of this form with federal, state and local income tax returns. Your employer must report employer contributions (which include pre-tax cafeteria plan deductions to income) to your HSA in Box 12 on your W-2 Form. This should be coded W according to the instructions.

Form 1040

US individual income tax return

Your Form 1040 contains a line where you can enter your post-tax HSA contributions to calculate your adjusted gross income. You must include any distributions that were not made for qualified medical expenses whether to you, your spouse or dependents as part of your adjusted gross income. You will be assessed a 20 percent penalty and be required to pay income taxes on non-qualified distributions.

Form 1099-SA

Distributions from an HSA, Archer MSA, Medicare+ Choice MSA or Medicare Advantage MSA

Your HSA custodian or trustee will report any HSA distributions to you and to the IRS on Form 1099-SA, which is why you need to be prepared to justify your spending as allowable under the law.

Form 5329

Additional taxes on qualified plans (including IRAs) and other tax-favored accounts

Filling out this form will help you determine if you made any contributions or distributions that might be outside the allowable limits for your HSA. If you have had a life event, such as a divorce, this form is a good worksheet for calculating whether your change in coverage caused any additional tax liabilities.

If completion of this form shows that you owe any tax or penalties on non-qualified distributions or excess contributions, you must file this form with your income tax return.

Form 5498-SA

HSA, Archer MSA, Medicare+ Choice MSA or Medicare Advantage MSA information

Your HSA trustee or custodian must report contributions to the HSA to the IRS and to you on this form. Any amounts reported on Forms 1099-SA or 5498-SA should agree with what you report on your Form 1040.

Form 8889

HSA

You must file Form 8889 with your Form 1040 or Form 1040NR if you (or your spouse, if married and file a joint return) had any activity in your HSA during the year. You must file the form even if only your employer or your spouse's employer made contributions to the HSA.

You must complete a separate Form 8889 for each HSA if, during the tax year, you are the beneficiary of two or more HSAs, or you are a beneficiary of an HSA and you have your own HSA. Enter "statement" at the top of each Form 8889 and complete the form as instructed. Next, complete a controlling Form 8889 combining the amounts shown on each of the statement Forms 8889. Attach the statements to your tax return after the controlling Form 8889. If you and your spouse both have HSAs, you will need to complete a Form 8889 separate from your spouse's. There is no joint Form 8889 (instructions to Form 8889).

CHAPTER 10
Guidelines for employers

Why are insurance rates increasing so rapidly?

Most employers who do not have the majority of their employees in HSA-type plans continue to see significant insurance rate premium increases. In contrast, employers who have HSAs in place for their employees tend to see lower rate increases.

Industry studies suggest that more employers are turning to HSA-type plans to save money and help them be compliant with health reform requirements.

Healthcare costs are escalating for many reasons

- New technologies and treatments that increase life expectancy

- Rising numbers of patients with chronic illnesses

- Patients' failure to seek lower-cost options (such as generic drugs that may be as effective as brand-name medicines)

- Over-utilization of healthcare facilities (such as emergency rooms for minor illnesses)

- Administrative waste

- State and federal government mandates for extended coverage

Some of the drivers for healthcare costs are out of employers' control. However, other factors, such as influencing healthcare usage patterns, helping prevent chronic diseases through wellness programs, and lowering the average cost of claims offer possibilities for flattening the trend of rising insurance rates by rewarding positive employee behavior.

Poor visibility of costs

In many ways, our healthcare system does not make a direct connection between receiving a service and paying for it. Instead, a third party—the insurance company, employer or plan administrator—actually processes and pays the bill. The consumer seldom pays attention to the actual price tag.

The consumer is usually only impacted by the amount of his or her co-payment, rather than the full price for office visits, lab tests, etc. The consumer sees the co-payment as the price.

But as services become more expensive, the consumer pays for the increase indirectly through higher premium deductions from wages. The result is that premium costs are putting healthcare out of reach for employers and individuals.

How can an HSA improve the situation?

An HSA-qualified HDHP can bring both consumer choice and flexibility back into healthcare by increasing incentives for consumers to compare costs and demand better value.

Adding the ability to save on taxes and keep some of the savings achieved by careful consumerism provides even more incentive for consumers to take an active role in controlling healthcare costs.

A win-win for employers and employees

An HSA-qualified health plan gives employers an opportunity to empower employees to take control of the way they consume healthcare services. This can, in turn, lower the average cost of claims through better utilization of healthcare services and help lower your premium costs.

Many employers use the savings achieved through HSA strategies to fund additional benefit offerings for their employees or to retain staff they might otherwise lose due to downsizing.

The key to HSA success

Some studies show that employers receive the most significant benefits from their HSA strategy once HSA adoption exceeds 50 percent among the eligible employee population. At that point, the behavior change that affects utilization patterns and average cost of claims reaches critical mass and employers find they have more bargaining power to ask for lower rates from their insurance carriers. Rate trend savings are augmented by additional savings in payroll taxes.

Gradual migration or full replacement?

Some employers choose to offer their employees a single choice in plans—an HDHP with an HSA. This full-replacement strategy escalates the achievement of HSA program objectives.

Other employers, concerned about possible employee backlash or loss of ability to attract top employee talent, choose a more gradual approach by offering multiple benefit plan choices that include an HSA-qualified HDHP option. They usually set an objective of full replacement within three to five years.

Many employers report that they have four primary motivators for adopting the full-replacement approach:

- Their premiums are increasing so quickly, they know they will soon have to start cutting benefits to keep costs low. They have no choice. The traditional low premium, low out-of-pocket plans are unsustainable.

- When they see potential savings modeled in cost projection tools, they conclude that earlier adoption launches a positive chain reaction. High HSA adoption rate ➔ lower premiums ➔ reduced cost trend ➔ more funds available for making contributions to employees' HSAs ➔ even higher HSA adoption.

- Once an employee population is full-replace HSAs, employers find cost ancillary services such as wellness, incentives, telemedicine and cost-transparency tools to be more widely adopted.

- Lower costs for employers and employees make it more likely that employers can avoid onerous taxes associated with the healthcare reform.

Calculating projected savings

In the following example, a company with 1,500 employees has an HSA adoption rate of eight percent its first year. Its starting trend is nine percent. The company gradually increases employee HSA adoption to 86 percent over five years. With the savings in taxes and insurance premiums, it is able to save **$8,694,730** net of HSA contributions by the fifth year.

HSA cost trend

Annual savings

By adopting a full-replacement strategy and starting with 74 percent adoption the first year of its HSA program, its projected savings over the five-year period increases to **$22,666,633**.

HSA trend cost

Annual savings

The faster full adoption can be realized, the sooner the HSA strategy can build savings for the employer and healthy HSA balances for employees—letting success build on success to meet full HSA program objectives.

Increasing adoption

Research is clarifying ways employers can hold down the rising insurance premium trend while shifting some of the premium cost savings to employees' HSAs. The sooner they adopt these ways, the more savings they achieve and the more benefits they can preserve for their employees.

Confronting perceived risk

HealthEquity, Inc., the nation's oldest and largest HSA non-bank custodian, has conducted research among its client base and concluded there are three main factors that influence an employee's decision whether or not to enroll in an HSA-qualified HDHP:

- **Personal and family health status**
  There is concern about the risk of having major healthcare expenses before the HSA has enough funds to cover the deductible.

- **Age (implying better health at a younger age)**
  There is a perception that HSA-qualified HDHPs are ideal only for younger, relatively healthy people.

- **Perceived relative financial value of the HDHP vs. the traditional plan**
  Employees are skeptical about their ability to build and keep a large enough balance to achieve significant financial benefit.

There is one overriding account holder concern—risk of exposure to high out-of-pocket costs. Balanced against the perceived safety of a traditional low-deductible health plan, it can be difficult to encourage adoption quickly enough to build traction under a HSA strategy.

Ways to increase adoption

The following chart shows the various steps a company can take to increase HSA adoption and the relative effectiveness of those steps.

HealthEquity HSA adoption best practices

1. Plan options

The single most effective way to encourage adoption is a full-replacement approach that offers only one plan option—the HSA-qualified HDHP. This must be coupled with effective communication and financial incentives to build trust among employees.

HealthEquity's clients who have chosen to offer the full-replacement plan option report that a by-product of the approach is increased social networking among employees to comment on the plan and educate each other. On the other hand, client groups that have chosen the opposite approach, offering three or more plan options, report that their employees consistently remain with the same plans. HSA adoption among those groups remains at five percent or less.

High adoption	Full-replacement
Medium adoption	Dual option
Low adoption	3+ options

2. Employee premium differentials

When the premium of the HSA-qualified HDHP option is at least 40 percent less than other plan options, HSA adoption increases significantly.

High adoption	More than 40 percent differential
Medium adoption	15 percent - 39 percent differential
Low adoption	Less than 15 percent differential

3. Deductible level

One of the most effective ways to reduce the perception of risk is to keep the deductible as low as possible for the qualified HDHP. HealthEquity has observed that the majority of clients who have achieved high adoption (greater than 30 percent) set the deductible of the HDHPs to less than 2,000/4,000. They have coupled this with the lowest possible out-of-pocket maximum.

High adoption	Federally mandated minimum
Medium adoption	Up to $2,000/$4,000 single/family
Low adoption	More than $2,000/$4,000 single/family

4. Out-of-pocket maximum level

Another way to reduce risk for employees is to set the out-of-pocket maximum level for the HSA-qualified HDHP option equal to other plans offered to employees. Taking the risk away, then offering an employer contribution to the HSA has improved adoption rates even when two or more alternative plans are offered to employees during open enrollment.

High adoption	Equal alternative plan(s)
Medium adoption	Up to 50 percent higher than alternative plan(s)
Low adoption	Greater than 51 percent higher than alternative plan(s)

5. HSA employer contribution

Making a meaningful employer contribution to the employees' HSAs reinforces the win-win message of sharing the cost savings from a HSA plan. This has the greatest impact on HSA adoption.

The employer contribution also calls attention to the wealth-building aspect of an HSA-qualified HDHP and is a catalyst for social networking. Employees educate each other by discussing ways to build their balances and control costs.

It is also an important factor in reducing the perception of risk.

High adoption	Greater than 60 percent of deductible
Medium adoption	25 percent -59 percent of deductible
Low adoption	Less than 25 percent of deductible

6. Open enrollment

It is important to make it easy for employees to choose the HSA-qualified HDHP. Enrollment tools should be easy-to-use and understand.

If a menu of options is offered, it is more effective to have the HSA-qualified HDHP as the default choice.

High adoption	Active enrollment with HSA-qualified HDHP as default
Low adoption	Passive enrollment or active enrollment with non-HDHP default

7. Employee communication strategy

HealthEquity has noted that while all of the most successful client groups had a different mix of ways to achieve high HSA adoption rates and the resultant cost savings, there was one thing they all had in common: Active involvement of company executives in communication campaigns.

By starting early, participating in communication activities, and being vocal about their own enrollment in HSA-qualified HDHPs, executives were influential in building enthusiasm for HSA programs. They walked the walk to gain trust.

High adoption	Active communication campaign (six months in advance) with executive engagement
Medium adoption	Moderate specified communication campaign (two months in advance)
Low adoption	No or limited campaign

Way to achieve final success: Employee education

Education is key to a smooth transition to HSA-qualified health plans. Employees may be uncomfortable with this new type of plan, and many will not understand how it works.

For some who do not understand how the tax savings and premium decreases compare financially to a higher deductible, an HSA-qualified HDHP may look like a reduction in benefits.

In order to help employees get the most benefit from their HSAs, it is important that employers take the proper steps to help employees understand how the new plan works, how to contribute and how to make payments.

Employers need to help employees assess how much to contribute to an HSA, how to keep records, whom to ask when they have questions, how to check HSA balances, and how to use a network and get good healthcare information. The HSA administrator and health plan may have tools to help employers educate their employees.

Employers who provide employees with information and tools to help them make better healthcare decisions, especially decisions on how to use the healthcare system effectively, will see their employees taking full advantage of the opportunity to increase the equity in their accounts and gain every allowable tax benefit.

Employers and their HSA providers should also conduct employee education and communication activities throughout the plan year.

Rules for employers

A summary of rules that employers should follow to be fully compliant with the laws and regulations governing HSAs follows:

Comparability of contributions

(IRC Section 4980G and the regulations thereunder at Treas. Reg. Sec. 54.4980G)

Employer contributions to employees' HSAs must be comparable for all employees participating in the HSA. Comparability under IRS regulation requires the same dollar amount or the same percentage of the annual deductible amount for the HSA contribution. However, it is only necessary to count employees who are eligible individuals and have the same category of coverage (such as self-only or family) (Treas. Reg. Sec. 54.4980G-1 Q&A 2). Part-time employees (customarily those who are employed fewer than 30 hours per week) are tested separately (Treas. Reg. Sec. 54.4980G-3 Q&A 5). If the employer contributions fail the comparability test, an excise tax will be imposed on the employer equal to 35 percent of the amount the employer contributed to the HSA.

Unless it is done through a cafeteria plan, employers may not make matching contributions that are conditional on a contribution by the employee (Treas. Reg. Sec. 54.4980G-4 Q&A-8; Treas. Reg. Sec. 54.4980G-5). For example, through a cafeteria plan, an employer may offer to contribute $500 to your account on the condition that you also contribute to the account.

There is an exception to the comparability rule. Employers may contribute more to the HSAs of non-highly compensated employees. The IRS uses the same definition of highly compensated employees for HSAs that it uses for other retirement accounts (IRC Sec. 4980G(e), Treas. Reg. Sec. 54.4980G-6).

Notice requirement

Under the notice requirement, employers must notify employees that each eligible employee who establishes an HSA by the last day of February and notifies their employer will receive a comparable contribution to the HSA for the prior year. Employers will meet the notice requirement if, by January 15 of the following calendar year, they provide written notice to all affected employees (Treas. Reg. Sec. 54.4980G-4 Q&A 14).

Contribution requirement

Employers meet the contribution requirement for these employees if, by April 15 or an IRS-specified deadline, they contribute comparable amounts plus reasonable interest to the employees' HSAs for the prior year (Treas. Reg. Sec. 54.4980G-4 Q&A 2(f)).

Cafeteria plans (Treas. Reg. Sec. 54.4980G-5)

The comparability rules do not apply to contributions made through a cafeteria plan. Comparable participating employees in a cafeteria plan:

- Are covered by your HDHP and are eligible to establish an HSA.
- Have the same category of coverage (either self-only or family coverage).
- Have the same category of employment (part-time, full-time or former).

Excise tax (IRC Sec. 4980G, Treas. Reg. Sec. 54.4980G-1, Q&A 4)

If an employer made contributions to employees' HSAs that were not comparable, they must pay an excise tax of 35 percent of the amount contributed.

Employment taxes

Amounts employers contribute to their employees' HSAs are not generally subject to employment taxes (IRS Notice 2004-2 Q&A 19). Employers must report the contributions in box 12 on Form W-2 for each employee, including amounts the employee contributed through a cafeteria plan (Instructions to Form W-2. HSA contributions are coded W).

Employer contributions are deductible by the employer as contributions to a health plan.

Required reporting

There should be no surprises for the HSA owner. He or she should receive periodic statements on how much is in their HSA, how much it has earned in interest and investment returns, fees and administrative expenses (i.e. maintenance, check replacement), and expenses paid out of the HSA.

ERISA requirements for private employer plans

Two government agencies share most of the federal regulation of private employer benefit plans: the US Department of Labor and the IRS.

ERISA is the federal law that established legal guidelines for private employer benefit plan administration and investment practices. ERISA generally preempts state laws as they apply to private-sector employee benefit plans. For instance, state laws cannot be enforced against an employee benefit plan, even if the state law sets higher standards of benefits than available in the plan (ERISA Section 514, with the exception for HI's healthcare law enacted before 1974).

The Department of Labor enforces participants' benefit rights under ERISA, and the IRS makes sure employers meet the tax code rules that allow them to sponsor and deduct the costs of benefit plans.

HSAs pose new challenges to define and implement a health savings vehicle in an employment setting.

Unlike private employer's health plans, according to the Department of Labor (DOL Field Assistance Bulletin 2004-1, 2006-2), HSAs are not considered ERISA-covered employee benefit plans, as long as the employer's involvement is limited. Essentially, DOL created a safe harbor for HSA plans, meaning as long as these plans meet certain criteria, they are safe from classification as an employee benefit plan. Instead, an HSA is considered by DOL to be a personal healthcare savings vehicle, rather than group insurance.

This safe harbor exemption from ERISA for HSAs exists even if the employer makes contributions to the HSA, with the following caveats:

- The employer cannot limit the ability of eligible employees to move their funds to another HSA beyond the restrictions provided in the Internal Revenue Code (IRC).

- The employer may not impose conditions on utilization of HSA funds beyond restrictions permitted by the IRC.

- The employer cannot make or influence investment decisions with respect to funds contributed to the HSA.

- The employer cannot represent the HSA as an employee welfare benefit plan established or maintained by the employer.

- The employer may not receive any payment or compensation in connection with the HSA.

If an HSA meets these requirements, and therefore is not considered an ERISA plan, it is subject to state law.

Non-ERISA HSAs

An HSA that is not an ERISA plan—either because the employer made that choice or because the account holder did not obtain it through an employer—lacks a key protection other ERISA savings plans have.

Funds the account holder accumulates in an employer-sponsored pension plan are shielded from creditors in the event that the account holder declares personal bankruptcy. Because an HSA is not an ERISA plan, creditors can attach balances in the account to a bankruptcy.

Also, non-ERISA HSAs are subject to the states' unclaimed properties law (sometimes known as escheat laws). If your account is considered dormant for a period of time, the trustee or custodian must forward the amount to the State's treasury, which will hold it until the account owner claims it back. To prevent this, you will need to make sure your account is active by checking the balance periodically. Check with your custodian for the proper procedures for your state.

ERISA and governmental employer plans

Federal, state and local government employers are not subject to ERISA.

The Office of Personnel Management administers federal employee benefit laws. State and local government employees should look to the agencies charged with administering their benefit plans.

States and localities may vary widely on issues of reporting, comparability, eligibility, fiduciary obligations and recordkeeping.

CHAPTER 11
Federal and state HSA laws and healthcare reform

The federal HSA law

Section 1201 of the Medicare Prescription Drug Improvement and Modernization Act of 2003 was signed by President Bush on December 8, 2003 and became Public Law No: 108-173. This provision adds Section 223 to the IRC to permit eligible individuals to establish HSAs for taxable years beginning after December 2003.

On March 23, 2010, President Obama signed the Patient Protection and Affordable Care Act (PPACA). While PPACA addresses a lot more than HSAs, some of PPACA's new requirements for insurance coverage impact how HSAs are used.

State laws affecting HSAs

An HSA is a trust

A trust is a fiduciary relationship where a bank, corporation or other entity acting as a trustee holds legal title with a legal obligation to keep and use the trust for the benefit of the equitable owner.

A trustee is a party given legal responsibility to hold property in the best interest of or for the benefit of another entity or person. The trustee is responsible for managing and investing funds. A custodian on the other hand, is the person or institution in charge of property in terms of maintenance of an account, but with no investment or management responsibilities.

An HSA is a trust because it is owned by the account holder, accumulates funds year-to-year, and is governed by specific uses and rules. An HSA is subject to both state and federal law as a trust.

An HSA trustee must be a bank, insurance company, or a non-bank trustee (an entity that meets specific IRS requirements)(IRC Sec. 223(d)(1)(B)).

The trustee must deal with the trust property honestly, put the beneficiary's interest above its own and closely follow the terms of the trust. Though it may have discretion over investments and day-to-day management, these functions are still governed by the trust agreement. The benefit for which the trustee holds and administers an HSA is to pay for qualified medical expenses.

States define official establishment of a trust

Many state trust laws maintain that an HSA is established or "opened" once funds are deposited in the account.

States may have different rules regarding the establishment of trusts. For example, Utah passed a 2009 law that amended its trust law to allow greater flexibility when determining when an HSA is established. Utah allows the establishment of the HSA to coincide with the date the account holder enrolled in a federally qualified HDHP(UT Code Sec. 75-7-401(2)), provided that the account is opened no later than the filing deadline, without extensions, of the account owner's federal tax return.

State requirements for HDHPs and preventive care

State insurance laws often require health plans to provide certain healthcare benefits without regard to the deductible, or on terms no less favorable than other care provided by the health plan. For an HDHP to offer preventive care, the IRS defined (and continues to define under PPACA) standards for preventive care—what the plan can pay for without jeopardizing the plan's tax status—rather than adopting the criteria for preventive care applied under state law.

Federal law overlap with state law

A plan that meets federal law may not meet state requirements. In a state where insurance laws conflict with the federal law governing HSAs, you may not be able to enroll in an HSA unless it is combined with an employer's self-insured HDHP. Self-insured plans are governed by ERISA and do not have to comply with state benefit laws.

Exemptions from state mandates

State legislatures can decide how to best deal with HSAs. Some have enacted exemptions from state mandates for plans that meet federal criteria for HSA-qualified HDHPs.

As a rule of thumb, if your health plan or broker offers an HSA-qualified plan in your state, it is likely legal for you to purchase the plan and contribute to the account.

Different tax treatments

It is important to recognize that while an HSA is a pre-tax savings account under federal income tax laws, it may not qualify for tax breaks under state or local income tax laws, or under the state component of the tax that finances unemployment benefits. State tax law and state estate law may also affect how HSAs are treated.

How federal healthcare reform affects HSAs

When PPACA was signed into law in 2010, many HSA enthusiasts were concerned that the new law would undermine the success of HSAs. While PPACA is a very complex law with a number of moving parts, many of the outstanding issues have been addressed with regulations, that in most cases appear to work well with and are even quite friendly to HSAs.

A number of these PPACA provisions, including waving pre-existing condition exclusions, removing lifetime and annual coverage maximums, providing first-dollar coverage for preventive care, and changes in purchasing over-the-counter (OTC) medications are discussed below, along with their impact on HSAs and other healthcare accounts. These provisions of the law are discussed in order of the year in which they became effective.

2014 to 2017

Health insurance exchanges in each state provide insurance to individuals and small groups

Most states have set up a network of health insurance exchanges. These exchanges enable people to comparison shop for standardized health packages. Often times, HSA-qualified health plans will be the least expensive plans on these exchanges. The healthcare reform law will facilitate enrollment and administer tax credits, so that people of all incomes can obtain affordable coverage.

Starting in 2014, most individuals were required to obtain an acceptable level of health insurance coverage or pay a penalty.

The penalty for not having coverage was $95 in 2014, $325 in 2015, $695 or up to 2.5 percent of income in 2016 and 2017, up to a cap of the national average bronze plan premium (IRC Section 5000A). Families paid half the amount for children, up to a cap of $2,250 per family.

However, on December 19, 2017, Congress passed the Tax Cut and Jobs Act of 2017 that abolished the Affordable Care Act's penalty for not having health insurance in 2019 and beyond.

The law does not technically eliminate the requirement that individuals have healthcare coverage, but the IRS will no longer seek to collect the penalty from individuals who do not have health insurance in 2019.

All non-grandfathered coverage that is purchased by individuals from insurance companies or through exchanges, or that is offered by small employers to their employees, must meet minimum standards in order to be deemed essential health benefits (EHBs) (Section 1302 of the Affordable Care Act). EHBs include coverage for 10 general areas of health services, including:

- Ambulatory patient services
- Emergency services
- Hospitalization
- Maternity and newborn care
- Mental health and substance abuse disorder services
- Prescription drugs
- Rehabilitative and habilitative services and devices
- Laboratory services
- Preventive and wellness services and chronic disease management
- Pediatric services, including oral and vision care

Beginning in 2014, EHBs have cost-sharing limits for deductibles ($2,050 single/$4,100 family for 2015) and in-network, out-of-pocket maximums ($6,350 single/$12,700 family for 2015). EHBs must also meet 60 percent actuarial value (AV) requirements—meaning that the plan must pay for at least 60 percent of the cost of care that would be covered by a plan that had no out-of-pocket cost-sharing requirement.

Federal regulations have confirmed that employers' contributions to HSAs will positively affect the AV calculation by counting toward the 60 percent requirement (Section 1302(d)(2)(B) of the Affordabe Care Act, 45 CFR 156.140(c)). By definition, EHBs can be HSA-qualified and still meet the minimum PPACA standards. Many employers are better understanding that HSA-based health plans can meet the PPACA EHB requirements, while still being cost effective for them and their employees through helping their employees avoid taxes by saving with their HSAs.

Insurers will no longer be able to exclude coverage for treatments based on pre-existing health conditions. Insurers are also prohibited from charging higher rates due to health status, gender or other factors.

Starting in 2014, requirements apply to all health plans. All grandfathering or exceptions will be eliminated. Premiums will vary only on age (no more than 3:1), geography, family size and tobacco use.

Annual limits on the amount of coverage an individual receives eliminated

Elimination of annual limits started with some plans in 2010. In 2014, it applied to all major medical health plans (excluding gap or mini-med plans) without exception. This eliminates the need to pay for supplemental coverage from an HSA or other healthcare account.

Insurance companies will not be able to drop an individual from coverage for routine care if the individual is enrolled in a clinical trial

As of 2014, PPACA prohibits insurers from dropping coverage because an individual chooses to participate in a clinical trial, in addition to denying coverage for routine care that they would be covered otherwise. This applies to all clinical trials that treat cancer and other life-threatening diseases.

Until in effect, your healthcare account is an important safety net for you. If you have to pay for coverage out-of-pocket while in a clinical trial, you at least reduce some of the costs by paying with tax-free dollars.

2022

An excise tax of 40 percent (Cadillac Tax) applies to excess premiums for high-cost health plans (IRC Sec. 4980 I)

A 40 percent excise tax will be charged to employers for annual healthcare spending above $10,200 for individuals or $27,500 for families. The Cadillac Tax healthcare spending calculation is expected to include the following:

- All employer and employee insurance premium costs, including administrative fees
- All employer and employee payroll contributions to FSAs, HSAs and HRAs
- Any tax-deductible, supplementary coverage purchased by employer or employee

Costs for stand-alone dental and vision plans are not expected to be included in the Cadillac Tax calculation. The Cadillac Tax thresholds are expected to increase by an inflation adjustment each year, and adjustments will also be made to increase the thresholds for employers with higher-risk occupations or an older workforce. While these thresholds may seem high, medical costs continue to increase rapidly and PPACA adds even more costs to premiums. Some estimates suggest that at current trends, as many as 60 percent of employers will be subject to some Cadillac Tax by 2022 for exceeding the threshold.

While HSA and other health account contributions will be included in the Cadillac Tax calculations, HSA plans are generally lower cost and can help employers avoid the Cadillac Tax penalties. As employers begin to increase deductibles and other cost sharing in an effort to avoid the Cadillac Tax that is scheduled to come into play in 2022, HSA account holders are wise to save as much money in their HSAs today to prepare for their future healthcare costs. HSAs provide the best tax-favored vehicle for Americans to save tax-free money for healthcare.

CHAPTER 12
Connecting Health and Wealth

Using an HSA to maximize your retirement benefits

For the first time ever, Americans can prepare not only for their future retirement needs, but also to create significant wealth by thoughtfully using their HSA alongside their 401(k) and other retirement accounts.

One of the many advantages of HSAs is that unused funds carry over every year for use in the future. These funds earn tax-free interest (in most cases) and any potential gains that come from investing the funds are also tax-free.

By strategically contributing to an HSA and other retirement accounts, you can further reduce taxes and supercharge your efforts to provide financial stability in your retirement years.

Introduction to standard retirement accounts

Funding retirement

There are many accounts and plans that people can use to save for retirement. Many of these retirement accounts are employer-sponsored plans funded through payroll deductions. IRAs and 401(k) plans have become the most common retirement savings accounts for Americans and it is likely that you are using one of these to prepare for your retirement.

Traditional IRAs

An individual retirement account (IRA), allows you to make tax-deductible contributions that, with some limitations, reduce your tax liability. Deductions depend on your income level and whether you are covered by a workplace retirement account.

IRAs allow an individual to avoid taxes on amounts contributed to the IRA and by enabling investments that can grow tax-deferred without capital gains or dividend income. Taxes on an traditional IRA are only paid when the money is withdrawn. You can begin making withdrawals without penalty, paying ordinary income taxes on distributions at age 59½. Withdrawals before age 59½ are subject to a 10% penalty in addition to ordinary income taxes.

Contribution limits to an IRA depend on tax filing status as well as income levels and age. You should consult a tax professional or a financial advisor to see how much you are eligible to contribute to an IRA. For 2018, the maximum IRA contribution amount (per person) is $5,500 each year ($6,500 if you are 50 or older). After age 70½, you can no longer contribute to a traditional IRA.

In addition, a traditional IRA has required minimum distributions (RMDs) once you reach age 70½. The RMD is determined annually based on your life expectancy. Failing to make an RMD is an expensive mistake that could lead to a 50% penalty plus taxes owed on the missed distribution.

Roth IRAs

The Roth IRA (named for Senator William Roth who helped establish the account in 1997), is similar to a traditional IRA but with a big difference in how the accounts are taxed.

Roth IRAs are funded using after-tax dollars, meaning contributions are not tax-deductible. However, once you begin withdrawing funds from the account, any distributions (including interest or earnings) are tax-free if the distribution comes at least five years after you established the account and at least one of the following has occurred:

- You are at least 59½ when the distribution occurs. All employer and employee payroll contributions to FSAs, HSAs and HRAs

- Funds are used to purchase (or build or rebuild) a first home for you or a qualified family member (a limit of $10,000 for this distribution is strictly enforced by the IRS)

- You became disabled

- Assets from the Roth IRA are distributed after your death

Failure to comply with these rules could lead to the distribution being subject to income tax as well as a 10% penalty.

Unlike traditional IRAs, you can contribute to a Roth IRA after age 70½ and you are not subject to required minimum distributions.

Contribution limits to Roth IRAs are the same as those for traditional IRAs.

401(k)s and 403(b)s

A 401(k) is the most common employer-sponsored retirement plan used today. A 403(b) is nearly identical to a 401(k) but it is used by non-profit or public institutions such as schools, charities and hospitals. There are other minor differences between these two retirement vehicles, but contribution limits and age requirements are the same for both.

A 401(k) or 403(b) allows you and/or your employer to contribute a portion of your wages to an account specifically designed for retirement. Most contributions are made pre-tax, income and growth accumulate tax-deferred and distributions are considered taxable income.

Similar to IRAs, your maximum contribution limit depends on your age and income level as well as possible other factors. In 2018, an employee can contribute up to $18,500 each year to their 401(k) or 403(b) ($24,500 for those 50 and older) depending on their individual circumstances. Employers can also contribute up to $36,500 to an employee's 401(k) depending on that employee's individual circumstances. The maximum combined employee and employer contribution to an employee's 401(k) or 403(b) in 2018 is $55,000. A tax advisor or financial planner can help you calculate what your maximum contribution limit is based on your individual circumstances.

Contribution limits to a 401(k) or 403(b) for 2019 have not been announced as of the printing of this edition of the Guidebook. The IRS generally announces the next year's 401(k) and 403(b) contribution limits in October.

The IRS limits how and when you can withdraw funds from your 401(k) or 403(b). Taking funds from the account too early can lead to significant tax penalties. You are also subject to required annual minimum distributions based on your age, retirement date and other factors.

NOTE:

The previous section regarding retirement plans is intended as a general introduction only. If you would like to learn more about these or any other types of retirement plans, such as SIMPLE IRAs and SEP IRAs, it is recommended that you seek out more information from a tax advisor, certified financial planner (CFP) or any number of books written specifically about these types of retirement accounts. The remainder of this chapter will discuss the tax and other advantages of HSAs and how you can use these benefits alongside an IRA or 401(k) or 403(b) to help you plan for retirement.

The remarkable tax benefits of HSAs

Pre-tax benefits of HSAs

Contributing funds to your HSA on a pre-tax basis is a benefit that can save you and your employer thousands of dollars over the life of the account on different federal and state taxes, including:

- Federal Insurance Contributions Act (FICA): FICA taxes are withheld from each paycheck you receive. The taxes include a 6.2% social security tax, a 1.45% Medicare tax and a 0.9% Medicare surtax if you earn over $200,000. Your employer also pays a 6.2% social security tax and a 1.45% Medicare tax.

  By contributing to your HSA pre-tax via payroll deductions, your income is reduced by the amount you pay to your HSA and reduces your and your employer's FICA tax obligation.

- Federal Unemployment Tax Act (FUTA): FUTA taxes are paid by your employer based on your wages. The first $7,000 you earn is taxed at 6.2%. The amount is not withheld from your wages.

  When you or your employer contribute to your HSA, it lowers the earnings used when calculating the employer-paid FUTA tax.

  State Unemployment Tax ACT (SUTA): SUTA is a counterpart to FUTA but is a state tax instead of a federal one. Each state sets its own unemployment tax rate and wage base.

  When you or your employer contribute to your HSA pre-tax, it lowers the earnings used when calculating the employer-paid SUTA tax.

Contributing to an HSA also lowers your taxable income, which can help you save money each year when you file your federal and state income taxes.

The triple tax advantages of HSAs for healthcare spending

An HSA is the most tax-advantaged account in America today. In fact, an HSA offers three specific tax benefits that will save you money. The triple tax advantages of HSAs include:

1. **Contributions to your HSA are tax-free.** As stated previously, pre-tax contributions lower your taxable income and other tax obligations. If your employer contributes to your HSA, they can also reduce their taxable income and also deduct the contributed amount on their taxes.

2. **Any earnings or growth within the account is tax-free.** Funds accumulated in your HSA may be allocated to interest bearing investment vehicles or to mutual funds. HSA providers offer different interest rates and investment options, so it is a good idea to find a provider with options that are best suited to your financial objectives.

3. **When funds are used to pay for qualified medical expenses, the distribution of both principal and interest/growth is tax-free.** For a list of what is and what is not considered qualified medical expenses, please see Appendix B.

This triple tax advantages of HSAs means that if you use HSA funds as intended, you will not pay any taxes on the funds at all. If you use HSA dollars for anything other than qualified medical expenses before the age of 65, you will pay income taxes on the amount of your withdrawals and an additional 20% tax penalty.

Non-healthcare retirement spending

At age 65, you are allowed to spend your HSA funds on any expense. If the funds are used to pay for qualified medical expenses, you still won't have to pay taxes on distributions. If the money is used to pay for anything other than a qualified medical expense, you will have to pay income taxes on the distribution but you won't have to pay a tax penalty. In this way, an HSA is a type of retirement plan that, when used alongside an IRA or 401(k) or 403(b), can help you augment your savings for retirement.

The power of compound interest

HSAs are uniquely powerful in generating benefits from compound interest because of their triple-tax advantage. The tax-free amounts you contribute and keep in your HSA can lead to big gains over time because of compound interest, so it is a good idea to understand this principle so you can take advantage of it with your HSA.

In short, compound interest is calculated on the initial principal and also the accumulated interest of previous periods (interest earned on interest). Various factors determine how much can be earned with compound interest, but generally, the higher the number of compounding periods, the higher the interest you will earn.

This means that the more money you contribute to and keep in your HSA, the more money you can earn over time. And the longer you keep the money in the account, the more powerful the effect of compound interest.

Example

Compound interest can dramatically increase savings

John has an HSA-qualified high-deductible health plan and, after medical expenses, is able to make a net contribution of $3,000 each year in his HSA. If John saves that same amount every year for 30 years but doesn't invest those dollars to leverage the power of compound interest, John would accumulate $90,000 over a 30-year period. However, if John invests his contributions each year in a diversified investment portfolio and is able to achieve a 7% rate of return, his savings will have grown to over $303,000. That is $213,000 more than the actual amount he invested over that period of time.

Thoughtful funding of HSAs alongside other retirement accounts

Hierarchy of funding

One of the best ways to take advantage of your HSA and retirement plan is to fund both accounts in such a way that you receive the full benefits of both. Consider the following:

1. **Remember** that an HSA has superior tax benefits for any money that you will need to spend on healthcare in your future, and an HSA can be used after the age of 65 for non-healthcare spending. At that time, it will be subject to the same tax consequences as traditional IRAs and 401(k)s/403(b)s.

2. **Determine** if your employer is willing to contribute any funds to either your HSA or other retirement accounts, the level of this contribution and if a match is required to obtain the employer funding. It is usually a good idea to make sure you get your full employer contribution.

3. **Think** about the total amount of money that you have in your budget in any given year to contribute collectively to ALL of your retirement accounts.

Considering these factors, a thoughtful hierarchy of funding strategy may be to:

FIRST contribute enough money to your HSA and other retirement accounts to capture your employer's matching funding.

THEN contribute to your HSA up to the allowable annual maximum contribution, including catch-up contributions if they are available to you.

FINALLY, if you are able to contribute more money, contribute funds to non-HSA retirement funds that do not come with an employer match.

Different contribution strategies may work better for you based upon your tax status and individual circumstances, but we recommend that you discuss the hierarchy of funding strategy with your accountant or other tax professional.

Investing from your HSA

One great way to increase the earning potential of your HSA is to invest. Most HSA providers offer investment options after you have a certain amount of funds in your HSA (usually $1,000 or $2,000). Once you have accumulated the required balance in your HSA, you may choose to invest the excess in mutual funds, stocks and other investments, and any gains from those investments are not taxed.

HSA providers offer different investment options and benefits and charge different amounts when it comes to investing your HSA funds. Here are a few things to consider about when you are searching for the right HSA provider:

- Does the HSA provider offer advice on your investments, including automated advice? Automated advice (sometimes called 'robo-advice') is a way to manage investments using computer algorithms or other formulas. The algorithms are controlled by software and do not require a human financial adviser to manage the client's account or assets. If your HSA provider does provide automated advice, it is a good idea to ask how much this service costs and how successful the technology has been with returns on investments.

- How much does the HSA provider charge in investment-related fees? Different providers charge different fee amounts, and you will want to know exactly how much these fees are before choosing an HSA provider. Lower fees mean you will keep more of your investment earnings while higher fees could dramatically reduce your earnings over time. Companies such as Morningstar rank HSA providers based on fees and reviewing their findings can be a great way to find HSA providers with the lowest overall investment fees. Consider that funds typically carry underlying fees which should be considered in your evaluation of the overall cost of investing with a given provider.

- Balancing HSA investments with other retirement account investments can help diversify your portfolio and reduce investment risks.

Saving HSA funds for the future

Employees of all ages should start taking advantage of this retirement strategy

It's never too early or too late to start thinking about retirement. If you are young and just starting out in your career, thinking of your HSA as type of retirement vehicle and contributing with that mindset means you have the potential to save hundreds of thousands of dollars in your HSA that is ready to help meet your financial objectives when you retire.

If you are close to retirement and just now discovering the usefulness of an HSA combined with a retirement plan, know that there is still time for you to take advantage of the benefits that come from using your HSA as another retirement vehicle.

APPENDIX A
Glossary of health insurance terms

Above-the-line deduction. A deduction that can be taken from gross income before arriving at adjusted gross income (AGI). Examples include IRA contributions, HSA contributions, half of the self-employment tax, the self-employed health insurance deduction and alimony. The term is derived from a solid bold line on Form 1040 and 1040A above the line for adjusted gross income. A taxpayer can take deductions above the line and still choose whether to claim the standard deduction or itemize deductions.

Annual limit. A dollar limit on the claims an insurer will pay over the course of a plan year. The Patient Protection and Affordable Care Act (PPACA) prohibits annual limits for essential benefits for plan years beginning after September 23, 2010.

Authorization. A health insurance plan's permission to proceed with a medical or surgical procedure.

Balance billing. A bill that the participant receives for the portion of an out-of-network provider's bill that the insurance plan doesn't cover.

When a participant receives services from a healthcare provider that doesn't participate in the insurer's network, the healthcare provider isn't obligated to accept the insurer's payment as payment in full, and they can bill the participant for the unpaid amount.

Cafeteria plan. An employee benefit plan that allows employees to choose benefits from among a number of different options; including pensions, FSAs, health insurance, other insurance and paid time off.

Calendar year. January 1 to December 31 of the same year. The calendar year may be different than the plan year; the latter may be any 12-month period established by an employer or insurer for managing the plan and accounting for benefit payments.

Certificate of coverage. Written evidence of prior health coverage—required under HIPAA—and provided by the insurer once coverage ends.

An enrollee may need to provide this certificate to be exempt from limitations on coverage for pre-existing conditions. In most situations, PPACA has eliminated the need for this certificate by prohibiting denial of coverage for pre-existing conditions.

Chronic condition. A condition that lasts indefinitely, or recurs frequently, and can be treated, but not cured.

COBRA. Acronym for the Consolidated Omnibus Budget Reconciliation Act of 1985 that provides for the temporary continuation of group health plan coverage after a qualifying event to certain employees, retirees and family members who are qualified beneficiaries. An HSA can be used to pay for COBRA premiums.

Coinsurance. The percentage of an insurance claim for which the patient is responsible to pay.

Comparable contributions. Employer contributions are considered comparable if the employer makes similar contributions on behalf of all eligible employees with similar coverage during the same period. Contributions are considered comparable if either the same dollar amount or the same percentage of the deductible under the HDHP.

Conversion coverage. Coverage under an individual insurance policy when group health plan benefits are lost. Employers that offer an individual conversion option to active employees must make that option available to COBRA-qualified beneficiaries as well.

Contribution (for HSA). Deposit to the health savings account (HSA).

Co-payments. Fixed-dollar payments the patient makes for a doctor visit or prescription. For example, many HMOs and PPOs impose a co-payment (sometimes referred to as a co-pay) for an in-network doctor's visit.

Covered services. The medically necessary treatments a plan pays for, at least in part.

Custodian. An entity responsible for the maintenance or administration of an account (such as an HSA or IRA), but has no investment or management responsibilities.

Deductible. The amount of covered expenses that an individual pays for out-of-pocket before payments are made by the health plan.

Dependent.
For a health plan: A dependent that a health insurance company covers under an individual's health plan; not the same as a tax dependent.

In most cases, the health insurance company and state law decide who is a qualified dependent under the health plan. One exception is the federal mandate under PPACA that adult children up to age 26 be covered by a parent's family plan if the child doesn't have access to health coverage from his or her own employer. This coverage is not taxable to the parent. However, the child can only receive distributions from the parent's HSA if the child also qualifies as a tax dependent on the parent's return. If the adult child is covered under a parent's family HDHP, but doesn't qualify as a tax dependent, the child can open his or her own HSA.

For tax purposes: A person who can be claimed as a dependent on your federal tax return. This isn't the same as a dependent on your health plan. You can receive distributions from your HSA for qualified medical expenses paid only for your spouse and people you can claim as dependents on your tax return, whether or not they are covered by your family HDHP.

Distribution (for HSA). Withdrawal from a health savings account (HSA).

Eligible individual (for HSA). An individual who meets all the IRS criteria for contributing to his or her own HSA.

Emergency. The sudden onset of a condition or an accidental injury requiring immediate medical or surgical care to avoid permanent disability or death.

Employee assistance plan/program (EAP). An employee benefit that covers all or part of the cost for employees to receive counseling, referrals and advice in dealing with stressful life issues.

ERISA (Employee Retirement Income Security Act). A federal law that governs private-sector employee benefits plans.

Excess contribution (for HSA). An HSA contribution that's higher than allowed by the IRS.

Exchange. A government-regulated marketplace of insurance plans with different tiers, or levels of coverage, offered to individuals without healthcare or to small companies; also referred to as health exchange.

PPACA created new American Health Benefit Exchanges in each state to assist individuals and small businesses with comparing and purchasing qualified health insurance coverage.

Exclusions. Medical services or conditions for which a particular healthcare plan or policy won't pay.

First-dollar coverage. Benefits that pay the entire covered or eligible amount without requiring a deductible.

Flexible spending account (FSA). An arrangement that allows employees to set aside pre-tax earnings to pay for expenses not covered by their insurance or benefit plans. May be free-standing or part of a cafeteria plan. All unspent funds are forfeited back to the employer at the end of the year unless the employer allows a rollover.

Formulary. The list of drugs covered fully or in part by a health plan.

Full contribution rule. Also last-month rule. See last-month rule and testing period.

Gatekeeper. The doctor, usually a primary care doctor, pediatrician or internist, responsible for overseeing and coordinating all aspects of a patient's care.

In an HMO, the gatekeeper must preauthorize all referrals, except emergencies.

Grace period (for FSA). The period when the account holder can continue to incur expenses and submit reimbursements after the end of the plan year. After the end of the grace period, any unused balances for the previous plan year are forfeited back to the employer.

Grandfathered plan. A health plan that an individual was enrolled in prior to the passage of PPACA on March 23, 2010.

Grandfathered plans are exempt from many of the immediate changes required by PPACA. New employees may be added to group plans that are grandfathered, and new family members may be added to all grandfathered plans.

Healthcare reform law. See Patient Protection and Affordable Care Act (PPACA).

Health Insurance Portability and Accountability Act (HIPAA). A federal law that limits the exclusion of pre-existing conditions, permits special enrollment when certain life or work events occur, prohibits discrimination against employees and dependents based on health status, and guarantees availability and renewability of health coverage to certain employees and individuals. It also establishes strict standards for using and sharing private health information (PHI).

Health reimbursement arrangement (HRA). Sometimes called health reimbursement account. An employer-owned and funded account from which the employee is reimbursed for qualified medical expenses; such as co-payments, deductibles, vision care, prescriptions, long-term care, medical insurance and most dental expenses. Reimbursements aren't taxed to the employee and are deductible by the employer.

High-deductible health plan (HDHP). A type of health insurance plan that, compared to traditional health insurance plans, requires higher initial out-of-pocket spending, although premiums may be lower.

HIPAA. See Health Insurance Portability and Accountability Act (HIPAA).

HMO (health maintenance organization). A corporate entity (for-profit or not-for-profit) that provides or arranges for coverage of certain health services for a fixed, prepaid premium.

Home healthcare. Skilled nursing and related care supplied to a patient at home.

Hospice care. Care given to terminally ill patients, generally those with six months or less to live and that emphasizes meeting emotional needs and coping with pain. Care may be given in the patient's home or at a facility.

Hospital outpatient department. A facility or area where a range of non-urgent medical care is provided under the supervision of a physician.

Indemnity plan. A plan that pays health insurance benefits in the form of cash payments rather than services.

Individual coverage requirements and penalties. Requirement for most individuals to obtain acceptable health insurance coverage or pay a penalty. There will be no penalty if affordable coverage is not available to an individual.

Individual retirement account (IRA). An account that allows individuals to save for retirement on a tax-deferred basis. The amount that is tax deductible varies according to an individual's pension coverage, income tax filing status and adjusted gross income.

In-network provider. A healthcare provider (such as a hospital or doctor) contracted to be part of the network for a managed care organization (such as an HMO or PPO). The provider agrees to the managed care organization's rules and fee schedules in order to be part of the network and agrees not to balance-bill patients for amounts beyond the agreed upon fee.

Last-month rule. IRS rule that allows a participant who enrolls in a qualifying HDHP mid-year to contribute the entire yearly maximum contribution for his or her age and coverage level if the participant is HSA-eligible with an HDHP on the first day of the last month of the tax year (December 1 for most tax payers). Also referred to as the full contribution rule.

The participant must remain eligible for the entire testing period to avoid incurring taxes and penalties. See testing period.

Life event. A change in a participant's personal situation that results in the gain or loss of eligibility for an HSA, a health plan, or a spouse's or dependent's employer's plan.

If a participant experiences a qualified life event, he may be eligible to make changes to his benefit coverage. Some common life events include, but aren't limited to:

- Marriage or beginning of a domestic partnership
- Divorce or termination of a domestic partnership
- Birth or adoption of a child
- Death of a spouse or domestic partner or child
- Spouse's loss of coverage
- Child's loss of eligibility
- Change in employment status
- Loss of qualified HDHP coverage

Lifetime limit. The limit many health insurance plans place on the claims that the insurer will pay over the course of an individual's life.

PPACA prohibited lifetime limits on benefits beginning September 23, 2010.

Limited benefits plan. A type of health plan that provides coverage for only certain specified healthcare services or treatments or provides coverage for healthcare services or treatments for a certain amount during a specified period.

Managed care plan. A health plan that limits costs by limiting the reimbursement levels paid to providers and by monitoring healthcare utilization by participants or both.

Mandated benefit. A requirement in state or federal law that all health insurance policies provide coverage for a specific healthcare service.

Matching contributions. Employer contributions paid to the employee's account (HSA, FSA) only if the employee also contributes a minimum specified amount.

Medicare. A federal government health insurance program for people 65 and older, the disabled, and people with end-stage renal disease who require dialysis or a transplant; part of the Social Security system.

- **Medicare Part A.** Pays for inpatient hospital stays, care in a skilled nursing facility, hospice care and some home healthcare.

- **Medicare Part B.** Helps pay for doctors' services, outpatient hospital care, durable medical equipment and some medical services not covered by Part A.

- **Medicare Part C (Medicare Advantage Plans).** A combination of Part A and Part B. The main difference in Part C is that it's provided through private insurance companies approved by Medicare.

- **Medicare Part D.** A stand-alone prescription drug coverage insurance.

Medicare Part D "donut hole." The gap between the maximum spending amount Medicare Part D will cover and the minimum spending amount to qualify for catastrophic prescription drug coverage. The beneficiary is responsible for 100 percent of all costs between these two amounts.

Medicare supplement (Medigap) insurance. Private insurance that supplements Medicare and Medicare Advantage Plans. It reimburses out-of-pocket costs not covered by Medicare and that are the beneficiary's share of healthcare costs.

A participant can't have an HSA if he or she also has Medigap insurance.

Medical loss ratio. The percentage of health insurance premiums spent by the insurance company on actual healthcare services rather than administrative costs.

PPACA requires that large group plans spend 85 percent of premiums on clinical services and other activities for the quality of care for enrollees. Small group and individual market plans must devote 80 percent of premiums to these purposes.

Medically necessary treatments. Treatments appropriate for the diagnosis, care, or treatment of a certain injury or condition. Check the plan's definition; whether or not a given service is covered may depend on where and by whom it is delivered.

Mistaken distribution (for HSA). Mistaken withdrawal from a health savings account (HSA), such as a non-qualified medical expense or an overpayment to a healthcare provider. A participant can avoid paying income tax and a 20 percent penalty on the amount by returning the money to the HSA administrator for redeposit into the HSA.

Multistate plan. A plan, created by PPACA and overseen by the U.S. Office of Personnel Management (OPM), that is scheduled to be available in every state through healthcare exchanges beginning in 2014.

Network plan. A plan that generally provides more favorable benefits for services provided by its network of providers than for services provided outside the network.

Open enrollment. A period of time during which employees may change health plans without incurring costs or penalties.

Out-of-network provider. A healthcare provider (such as a hospital or doctor) that is not contracted to be part of a managed care organization's network (such as an HMO or PPO).

Depending on the managed care organization's rules, an individual may not be covered at all or may be required to pay a higher portion of the total costs when he or she seeks care from an out-of-network provider. A health plan may disallow applying out-of-network provider costs to the deductible.

Out-of-pocket limit. A maximum limit on the out-of-pocket expenses a participant pays during the plan year. Amounts a participant pays for deductibles, co-payments or coinsurance are included in out-of-pocket expenses and kept as a running total. Insurance premiums aren't counted toward out-of-pocket limits.

Once a participant reaches the plan's limit for the year, remaining eligible expenses are covered at 100 percent regardless of the plan's co-payment or coinsurance arrangements. Some plans refer to this limit as the stop-loss limit or out-of-pocket maximum.

Patient Protection and Affordable Care Act (PPACA).
Legislation (Public Law 111-148) signed by President Obama on March 23, 2010. Commonly referred to as the healthcare reform law.

Permitted coverage. Coverage an individual may maintain, in addition to an HDHP, without losing eligibility for an HSA, even though the coverage may provide first-dollar coverage for certain medical expenses.

PHI. Protected health information that is strictly protected by HIPAA.

Plan administrator. The person or firm designated by a health plan or employer to handle day-to-day details of recordkeeping, claims handling, and report filing.

Plan participant or beneficiary. An employee or dependent of that employee who is participating in, receiving benefits from, or eligible to receive benefits from an employee benefit plan.

Plan year. The calendar year (January 1 to December 31), or another 12-month period the employer or insurer chooses for managing a health plan and keeping track of deductibles and other limits.

Point of service (POS). A managed care plan that allows patients to see doctors not included in the plan, but for an increased fee; usually found as part of an HMO.

Portable account. An account that can be carried from job to job and from group plans to individual coverage.

Pre-existing condition exclusion. A period of time when an individual receives no benefits under a health benefit plan for an illness or medical condition for which the individual received medical advice, diagnosis, care or treatment within a specified period of time prior to the date of enrollment in the health benefit plan.

PPACA prohibits pre-existing condition exclusions for all plans beginning January 2014.

PPO (preferred provider organization). An arrangement between doctors and other medical service providers and an insurer to offer services at a discounted rate in exchange for the insurer sending patients to their doctors or facilities. Usually includes some utilization review.

Premium. The periodic payment required to keep an insurance policy in force.

Preventive benefits. Covered services intended to prevent or identify a medical condition while more easily treatable.

PPACA requires insurers to provide coverage for preventive benefits without charging deductibles, co-payments or coinsurance.

Primary payer. The healthcare plan that pays its share of covered expenses first when a consumer has access to two different health plans, while the secondary payer pays some or all of the amount left over—even if that amount is less than the secondary plan otherwise pays.

This applies to Medicare when the participant is still covered under an employer plan.

Prohibited transaction. The sale, exchange, or lease of property; borrowing or lending money; furnishing goods, services, or facilities; transferring to, used by, or for the benefit of the HSA account beneficiary of any assets contained in the account. Pledging account assets—as security for a loan, for example—constitutes a prohibited transaction.

Provider. Whoever provides healthcare under a health plan, including doctors, therapists, nurse-practitioners, and anyone else who provides medical services.

Provider discount. A reduced rate a doctor, hospital or other healthcare professional or facility agrees to accept when they enroll in a health plan's network.

Prudent layperson standard. Under this standard, emergency care is covered in a healthcare plan if the decision to go to the ER was one that an average person with average medical knowledge would make at the time.

Qualified health plan. A health insurance policy sold through an exchange.

PPACA requires exchanges to certify that qualified health plans meet minimum standards outlined in the law.

Qualified medical expense. An expense paid by the account beneficiary or owner, his or her spouse, or dependents, for medical care as defined in section 213(d) of the Internal Revenue Code; generally the same expense that individual taxpayers can deduct on federal income tax returns.

Certain types of health insurance premiums are considered a qualified medical expense for purposes of HSAs.

Referral. A recommendation of a medical professional. In HMOs and other managed care plans, a referral is usually necessary to see any practitioner or specialist other than a gatekeeper physician, for the service to be covered.

Release. Permission for specified medical information to be released to a specific person or entity.

Repricing. The adjustment of healthcare providers' "sticker price" to reflect discounts the providers may have negotiated with a health plan.

Rescission. The process of voiding a health plan from its inception usually based on the grounds of material misrepresentation or omission on the application for insurance coverage that would have resulted in a different decision by the health insurer with respect to issuing coverage. PPACA prohibits rescissions except in cases of fraud or intentional misrepresentation of a relevant fact.

Rollover contribution. Distribution of an account balance from one financial institution and redepositing it in another, or from one type of account (MSA) to another (HSA).

Safe harbor. When an activity is deemed to meet certain authorized criteria, it will be safe and considered in compliance with law or regulation.

Screening services. Medical tests designed to detect treatable diseases or conditions.

Section 401(k) plan. A defined contribution retirement plan that allows participants to have a portion of their compensation (otherwise payable in cash) contributed pre-tax to a retirement account on their behalf. The plan is named after the section of the Internal Revenue Code that establishes the rules for the plan.

Self-insured plan. A plan under which the employer pays for medical claims as they arise rather than contracting for coverage from an insurer.

Stop-loss limit. See out-of-pocket limit.

Testing period. The length of time an individual must remain in a qualified HDHP to avoid taxes and penalties if he/she makes the maximum yearly contribution to an HSA under the last-month rule.

If the individual enrolled in a qualifying HDHP mid-year, but contributed the full yearly maximum contribution to the HSA under the last-month rule, he/she must remain an eligible individual during the testing period. For the last-month rule, the testing period begins with the last month of the tax year and ends on the last day of the 12th month following that month. For example, December 1, 2018, through December 31, 2019. See last-month rule.

Transition rule. A gradual adaptation to a law in order to ease the impact of a change on affected tax payers.

Trend. Medical cost inflation; for example, the yearly increase in the cost of premiums.

Trust. Legal instrument allowing one party (the trustee) to control property for the benefit of another.

Trustee. An entity or individual that directs the investment of the funds in a trust account and has management responsibilities.

Umbrella deductible. A stated maximum amount of expenses a family could incur before receiving benefits.

Usual, customary and reasonable charge (UCR). The cost associated with a healthcare service that's consistent with the going rate for identical or similar services within a particular geographic area.

Reimbursement for out-of-network providers is often set at a percentage of the usual, customary and reasonable charge, which may differ from what the provider actually charges for a service.

Waiting period. A period of time that an individual must wait, either after becoming employed or submitting an application for a health insurance plan, before coverage becomes effective and claims may be paid.

Premiums aren't collected during this period, and HSA contributions can't begin until the first day of the month after the waiting period ends and HDHP coverage begins.

APPENDIX B
IRS forms

See www.irs.gov for full details.

US individual income tax return

- Form 1099-SA: www.irs.gov/pub/irs-pdf/ f1099sa.pdf

- Form W-2 (includes a section for HSA reporting): www.irs.gov/pub/irs-pdf/fw2.pdf

- Form 1040/1040EZ: www.irs.gov/pub/irs-pdf/f1040.pdf

Distributions from an HSA, Archer MSA, or Medicare Advantage MSA

- Form 5329: www.irs.gov/pub/irs-pdf/f5329.pdf

Additional taxes on qualified plans (including IRAs) and other tax-favored accounts

- Form 5498-SA: www.irs.gov/pub/irs-pdf/f5498sa.pdf

HSA, Archer MSA, or Medicare Advantage MSA information

- Form 5305b: www.irs.gov/pub/irs-pdf/f5305b.pdf

Health savings trust account

- Form 5305c: www.irs.gov/pub/irs-pdf/f5305c.pdf

For recent updates see www.hsaguidebook.com

APPENDIX C
Qualified medical expenses

The IRS provides yearly updates on the medical and dental expenses that are and are not tax-deductible. See www.irs.gov for the most current version of Publication 502—Eligible Medical and Dental Expenses.

The following is a list of items that can be included in figuring the medical expense deduction. Items are listed in alphabetical order and, if listed, the amount paid by a participant can be included as a medical expense.

Note: IRS Publication 502 discusses items that are eligible for tax deductions. Not all the items on this list may be reimbursed by an FSA, HRA or HSA. Each of those accounts has a subset of the list that is considered reimbursable, and the lists are not identical.

Qualified medical expenses:

Legal abortion.

Acupuncture.

Alcoholism. Inpatient treatment at a therapeutic center for alcohol addiction, including meals and lodging provided by the center during treatment; amounts paid for transportation to and from Alcoholics Anonymous meetings if attendance is pursuant to medical advice that membership in Alcoholics Anonymous is necessary for the treatment of patient's alcoholism.

Ambulance services.

Artificial limb.

Artificial teeth.

Autoette. See wheelchair.

Bandages.

Birth control pills.

Braille books and magazines. For use by a visually impaired person that is more than the cost of regular printed editions.

Breast reconstruction surgery. Following a mastectomy for cancer or other breast disease.

Capital expenses. Special equipment installed in a home and other home improvements if the main purpose is medical care for yourself, your spouse or your dependent. The cost of permanent improvements that increase the value of a property may be partly included as a medical expense. The cost of the improvement is reduced by the increase in the value of the property. The difference is a medical expense. If the value of the property is not increased by the improvement, the entire cost is included as a medical expense.

Certain improvements made to accommodate a home for a disabled person don't usually increase the value of the home, and the cost can be included in full as medical expenses. These improvements include, but aren't limited to, the following:

- Constructing entrance or exit ramps
- Widening doorways at entrances or exits
- Widening or otherwise modifying hallways and interior doorways
- Installing railings, support bars or other modifications to bathrooms
- Lowering or modifying kitchen cabinets and equipment
- Moving or modifying electrical outlets and fixtures
- Installing porch lifts and other forms of lifts (elevators generally add value to the house)
- Modifying fire alarms, smoke detectors and other warning systems
- Modifying stairways
- Adding handrails or grab bars anywhere (whether or not in bathrooms)
- Modifying hardware on doors
- Modifying areas in front of entrance and exit doorways
- Grading the ground to provide access to the residence

Only reasonable costs to accommodate a home for a disabled person are considered medical care. Additional costs for general repair or aesthetic reasons aren't medical expenses.

Example

Making capital improvements on a home

Stephen and Leslie are taking care of an elderly parent who has had a stroke. All the bedrooms and bathrooms in their home are on the second floor. They install an elevator and modify one bathroom to accommodate a wheelchair.

The elevator costs $8,000. An appraisal shows that the elevator increases the value of their home by $4,400.

They subtract the increased value of their home ($4,400) from the cost of the improvement ($8,000). The difference ($3,600) is the amount they can claim as a medical expense.

Construction to widen the doorway of a bathroom and replace the bathtub with a wheelchair-accessible shower costs $5,800. Because the bathroom remodel doesn't increase the value of their home, the owners can claim the entire $5,800 as a medical expense.

Operation and upkeep. Amounts paid for the operation and upkeep of a capital asset, as long as the main reason is for medical care; applies even if none or only part of the original cost of the capital asset qualify as a medical care expense.

Example

Improvements that increase the value of a home
If, in the previous example, the elevator increased the value of the home by $8,000, the owners wouldn't be able to claim any portion of the cost of the elevator as a qualified medical expense.

However, the cost of electricity to operate the elevator and any costs to maintain it are medical expenses as long as the medical reason for the elevator exists.

Improvements to property rented by a person with a disability. Amounts paid to buy and install special plumbing fixtures for a person with a disability (mainly for medical reasons) in a rented house are medical expenses.

Example

Improvements installed by a disabled tenant
John has arthritis and a heart condition. He can't climb stairs or get into a bathtub. On his doctor's advice, he installs a bathroom with a shower stall on the first floor of his two-story rented house.

The landlord didn't pay any of the cost of buying and installing the special plumbing and didn't lower the rent. John can include the entire amount he paid as a qualified medical expense.

Car. The cost of special hand controls and other special equipment installed in a car for the use of a person with a disability.

Car, special design. Difference between the cost of a regular car and a car designed to hold a wheelchair.

Car, transportation expenses. Out-of-pocket expenses, such as the cost of gas and oil, when a car is used for medical reasons are eligible. Depreciation, insurance, general repair, and maintenance expenses are not.

In lieu of actual expenses, a standard mileage rate for use of a car for medical reasons is eligible. To find the current mileage rate for medical treatment, go to www.irs.gov. Parking fees and tolls are eligible whether actual expenses or the standard mileage rate are used.

Chiropractor.

Christian Science practitioner.

Contact lenses. Needed for medical reasons (such as correcting vision or protecting the eye); cost of equipment and materials required for using contact lenses, such as saline solution and enzyme cleaner. See Eyeglasses and eye surgery.

Cosmetic surgery (reconstructive). If necessary to improve a deformity arising from, or directly related to, a congenital abnormality, a personal injury resulting from an accident or trauma, or a disfiguring disease.

Crutches. Purchase or rental.

Dental treatment. Includes fees paid to dentists for X-rays, fillings, braces, extractions, dentures, etc.

Diagnostic devices. For diagnosing and treating illness and disease, such as diabetic testing equipment and supplies.

Disabled dependent care expenses. Some may qualify as either medical expenses or work-related expenses for purposes of taking a credit for dependent care. This can be applied either way as long as you don't use the same expenses to claim both a credit and a medical expense deduction.

Drug addiction. Inpatient treatment at a drug treatment center, including meals and lodging.

Drugs. See medicines.

Eyeglasses. Needed for medical reasons; can also include fees paid for eye examinations.

Eye surgery. To treat illnesses, injuries and defective vision (laser eye surgery or radial keratotomy).

Fertility enhancement. Procedures such as in vitro fertilization (including temporary storage of eggs or sperm); surgery, including an operation to reverse prior surgery that prevented fertility.

Founder's fee. See lifetime care—advance payments.

Guide dog or other service animal. To be used by a visually-impaired or hearing-impaired person; the cost of a dog or other service animal trained to assist persons with other physical disabilities; amounts paid for the ongoing care of service animals.

Health institute. Only if prescribed by a physician, and the physician issues a statement that the treatment is necessary to alleviate a physical or mental defect or illness of the individual receiving the treatment.

Health maintenance organization (HMO). Premiums paid for yourself, your spouse or a dependent to receive medical care from a health maintenance organization. See insurance premiums.

Hearing aids. Also batteries to operate hearing aid.

Home care. See nursing services.

Home improvements. See capital expenses.

Hospital services. Cost of inpatient care at a hospital or similar institution if the principal reason for being there is to receive medical care; includes amounts paid for meals and lodging. Also see lodging.

Insurance premiums. HSA funds can be used to pay for insurance premiums under the following circumstances:

- You are collecting federal or state unemployment benefits.
- You have COBRA continuation coverage through a former employer.
- You have a qualified long-term care insurance contract (subject to additional limitations).

If you have a policy that provides more than one kind of payment, you can include the premiums for the medical care part of the policy if the charge for the medical part is reasonable. The cost of the medical part must be separately stated in the insurance contract or given to you in a separate statement.

Note: If advance payments of the health coverage tax credit are made on an individual's behalf to an insurance company, don't include any advance payments made when figuring the amount the individual may deduct for insurance premiums. Also, if this individual is claiming the health coverage tax credit, the individual can subtract the amount shown on line 4 of Form 8885 (reduced by any advance payments shown on line 6) from the total insurance premiums paid.

- **Medicare Part A premiums.** If covered under Social Security (or if a government employee who paid Medicare tax), an individual is enrolled in Medicare A. The payroll tax paid for Medicare A is not a medical expense.

  If the individual isn't covered by Social Security (or wasn't a government employee who paid Medicare tax), he/she can voluntarily enroll in Medicare A. In this situation the premiums the individual pays for Medicare A can be included as a medical expense on her tax return.

- **Medicare Part B premiums.** Medicare B is a supplemental medical insurance plan. Premiums paid for Medicare B are a medical expense.

  If an individual applied for Medicare B at 65 or after he became disabled, he/she can deduct the monthly premiums paid.

  If you were over 65 or disabled when you first enrolled, check the information you received from the Social Security Administration to find out your premium.

- **Medicare Part C (Medicare Advantage) premiums.**

- **Medicare Part D premiums.**

- **Prepaid insurance premiums.** Premiums paid before 65 for insurance for medical care for an individual, a spouse or dependents after an individual reaches 65 are medical care expenses in the year paid if:
  - Payable in equal yearly installments or more often.
  - Payable for at least 10 years, or until the individual reaches age 65 (but not for less than five years).

Glossary | 195

Laboratory fees. If part of medical care.

Lead-based paint removal. The cost of removing lead-based paints from surfaces in the home to prevent a child who has or had lead poisoning from eating the paint.

The surfaces must be in poor repair (peeling or cracking) or within the child's reach. The cost of repainting the scraped area isn't a medical expense.

If, instead of removing the paint, the area is covered with wallboard or paneling, treat these items as capital expenses. See capital expenses. The cost of painting the wallboard can't be included as a medical expense.

Learning disability. See special education.

Legal fees. To authorize treatment for mental illness.

Lifetime care—advance payments. Part of a life-care fee or founder's fee paid monthly or as a lump sum under an agreement with a retirement home.

The part of the payment included is the amount properly allocable to medical care. The agreement must require that an individual pay a specific fee as a condition for the home's promise to provide lifetime care that includes medical care.

An individual can use a statement from the retirement home to prove the amount properly allocable to medical care. The statement must be based either on the home's prior experience or on information from a comparable home.

- **Dependents with disabilities.** Advance payments to a private institution for lifetime care, treatment, and training a physically or mentally impaired child upon the caregiver's death or when the caregiver becomes unable to provide care. The payments must be a condition for the institution's future acceptance of the child and must not be refundable.

- **Payments for future medical care.** Generally, an individual can't include in medical expenses current payments for medical care (including medical insurance) to be provided substantially beyond the end of the year. This rule doesn't apply in situations where the future care is purchased in connection with obtaining lifetime care of the type described above (see dependents with disabilities).

Lodging. Cost of meals and lodging at a hospital or similar institution if a principal reason for being there is to receive medical care. See nursing home.

An individual may be able to include in medical expenses the cost of lodging not provided in a hospital or similar institution. The individual can include the cost of such lodging while away from home if all of the following requirements are met:

- The lodging is primarily for and essential to medical care.

- The medical care is provided by a doctor in a licensed hospital or in a medical care facility related to, or the equivalent of, a licensed hospital.

- The lodging isn't lavish or extravagant under the circumstances.

- There is no significant element of personal pleasure, recreation or vacation in the travel away from home.

The amount included in medical expenses for lodging can't be more than $50 for each night for each person. The individual can include lodging for a person traveling with the person receiving the medical care. For example, if a parent is traveling with a sick child, up to $100 per night can be included as a medical expense for lodging. Meals aren't included.

Don't include the cost of lodging while away from home for medical treatment if that treatment isn't received from a doctor in a licensed hospital or in a medical care facility related to, or the equivalent of, a licensed hospital or if that lodging isn't primarily for or essential to the medical care received.

Long-term care. Amounts paid for qualified long-term care services and premiums paid for qualified long-term care insurance contracts.

Long-term qualified care services. Necessary diagnostic, preventive, therapeutic, curing, treating, mitigating, rehabilitative services, and maintenance and personal care services (defined below) that are:

- Required by a chronically ill individual.

- Provided as the result of a plan of care prescribed by a licensed healthcare practitioner.

- **Chronically ill individual.** An individual is chronically ill if, within the previous 12 months, a licensed healthcare practitioner has certified that the individual meets either of the following descriptions:

  – He or she is unable to perform at least two activities of daily living without substantial assistance from another individual for at least 90 days, due to a loss of functional capacity. Activities of daily living are eating, toileting, transferring, bathing, dressing and continence.

  – He or she requires substantial supervision to be protected from threats to health and safety due to severe cognitive impairment.

- **Maintenance and personal care services.** Care that has as its primary purpose providing a chronically ill individual with needed assistance with his disabilities (including protection from threats to health and safety due to severe cognitive impairment).

Long-term qualified care insurance contracts. An insurance contract that provides only coverage of qualified long-term care services.

The contract must:

- Be guaranteed renewable.

- Not provide for a cash surrender value or other money that can be paid, assigned, pledged or borrowed.

- Provide that refunds, other than refunds on the death of the insured or complete surrender or cancellation of the contract, and dividends under the contract must be used only to reduce future premiums or increase future benefits.

- Generally not pay or reimburse expenses incurred for services or items that would be reimbursed under Medicare, except where Medicare is a secondary payer, or the contract makes per diem or other periodic payments without regard to expenses.

- **Qualified long-term care premiums**. Qualified long-term care premiums, up to the amounts shown below, can be included as medical expenses on Schedule A (Form 1040). The limit on premiums is for each person as of 2018:
    – Age 40 or under: $420
    – Age 41 to 50: $780
    – Age 51 to 60: $1,560
    – Age 61 to 70: $4,160
    – Age 71 or over: $5,200

- **Unreimbursed expenses for qualified long-term care services.**

Meals. The cost of meals at a hospital or similar institution if a principal reason for being there is to get medical care. The cost of meals that aren't part of inpatient care are ineligible.

Medical conferences. Amounts paid for admission and transportation to a medical conference if the medical conference concerns the chronic illness of an individual, a spouse or a dependent.

The costs of the medical conference must be primarily for and necessary to the medical care of an individual, a spouse or a dependent. The majority of the time spent at the conference must be spent attending sessions on medical information.

The cost of meals and lodging while attending the conference is not deductible as a medical expense.

Medical information plan. Amounts paid to a plan that keeps medical information in a computer data bank and retrieves and furnishes the information on request to an attending physician.

Medical services. Amounts paid for legal or medical services provided by:
- Physicians
- Surgeons
- Specialists
- Other medical practitioners

Medicare Part A: Covers hospital insurance that pays for inpatient hospital stays, care in a skilled nursing facility, hospice care and some home healthcare.

Medicare Part B: A medical insurance that helps pay for doctors' services, outpatient hospital care, durable medical equipment and some medical services that aren't covered by Part A.

Medicines. Medications prescribed by a provider to treat a specific medical condition.

Beginning January 1, 2011, over-the-counter medications (except insulin and medications prescribed by a provider) are only eligible for reimbursement from an HSA or other healthcare account.

Mentally challenged, special homes for. Costs of keeping a mentally challenged person in a special home, not the home of a relative, on the recommendation of a psychiatrist to help the person adjust from life in a mental hospital to community living.

Nursing home. Costs of medical care for an individual, a spouse or a dependent in a nursing home, home for the aged or similar institution.

This includes the cost of meals and lodging in the home if a principal reason is to get medical care.

If the reason for being in the home is personal, the cost of meals and lodging is ineligible.

Nursing services. Wages and other amounts paid for nursing services.

Services need not be performed by a nurse as long as the services are of a kind generally performed by a nurse. This includes services connected with caring for a patient's condition, such as giving medication or changing dressings, as well as bathing and grooming the patient. Services can be provided at home or a care facility.

Generally, only the amount spent for nursing services is a medical expense. If the attendant also provides personal and household services, amounts paid to the attendant must be divided between the time spent performing household and personal services and the time spent for nursing services. However, certain maintenance or personal care services provided for qualified long-term care can be included as medical expenses. Additionally, certain expenses for household services or for the care of a qualifying individual incurred to allow you to work may qualify for the child and dependent care credit (See IRS Publication 503—Child and Dependent Care Expenses).

Part of the amount paid for that attendant's meals is also eligible. Divide the food expense among the household members to find the cost of the attendant's food. Then divide that cost in the same manner as in the preceding paragraph. If additional amounts were paid for household upkeep because of the attendant, these amounts can be included. This includes extra rent or utilities paid because of a move to a larger apartment to provide space for the attendant.

- **Employment taxes.** Social Security tax, FUTA, Medicare tax, and state employment taxes paid for a nurse, attendant, or other person who provides medical care.

If the attendant also provides personal and household services, the amount of employment taxes paid for medical services as explained under nursing services is eligible. For information on employment tax responsibilities of household employers (see IRS Publication 926—Household Employer's Tax Guide).

Operations. Amounts paid for legal operations that aren't for unnecessary unprescribed cosmetic surgery.

Optometrist. See eyeglasses.

Organ donors. See transplants.

Glossary | 201

Osteopath.

Oxygen. Oxygen equipment to relieve breathing problems caused by a medical condition.

Prosthesis. See artificial limb.

Psychiatric care. Includes the cost of supporting a mentally ill dependent at a specially equipped medical center where the dependent receives medical care. See psychoanalysis and transportation.

Psychoanalysis.

Psychologist. Amounts paid for medical care.

Special education. Fees paid on a doctor's recommendation for a child's tutoring by a teacher who is specially trained and qualified to work with children with learning disabilities caused by mental or physical impairments, including nervous system disorders.

An individual can include as medical expenses the cost (tuition, meals and lodging) of attending a school that furnishes special education to help a child to overcome learning disabilities. A doctor must recommend that the child attend the school.

Overcoming the learning disabilities must be a principal reason for attending the school, and any ordinary education received must be incidental to the special education provided. Special education includes:

- Teaching braille to a visually impaired person.
- Teaching lip reading to a hearing impaired person.
- Giving remedial language training to correct a condition caused by a birth defect.

An individual can't include in medical expenses the cost of sending a problem child to a school where the course of study and the disciplinary methods have a beneficial effect on the child's attitude if the availability of medical care in the school isn't a principal reason for sending the student there.

Sterilization. Legally performed operation to make a person unable to have children.

Stop-smoking programs. Note that amounts paid for drugs that do not require a prescription, such as nicotine gum or patches, designed to help stop smoking, are ineligible.

Surgery. See operations.

Telephone. Cost of special telephone equipment that lets a hearing-impaired person communicate over a regular telephone; also the cost of repairing the equipment.

Television. Equipment that displays the audio part of television programs as subtitles for hearing-impaired persons; may be the cost of an adapter that attaches to a regular set or part of the cost of a specially equipped television that exceeds the cost of the same model regular television set.

Therapy. Received as medical treatment.

- **Patterning exercises**. For a mentally retarded child; must consist mainly of coordinated physical manipulation of the child's arms and legs to imitate crawling and other normal movements.

Transplants. Medical care received because an individual is a donor or possible donor of a kidney or other organ; and medical care of a donor in connection with the donating of an organ to another individual, including transportation.

- Transportation primarily for, and essential to, medical care, including: bus, taxi, train or plane fares or ambulance services.

- Transportation expenses of a parent who must go with a child who needs medical care.

- Transportation expenses of a nurse or other person who can give injections, medications or other treatment required by a patient who is traveling to get medical care and can't travel alone.

- Transportation expenses for regular visits to see a mentally ill dependent, if these visits are recommended as a part of treatment.

Transportation. You can include in medical expenses amounts paid for transportation primarily for, and essential to, medical care.

You can include:

- Bus, taxi, train or plane fares or ambulance service.

- Transportation expenses of a parent who must go with a child who needs medical care.

- Transportation expenses of a nurse or other person who can give injections, medications, or other treatment required by a patient who is traveling to get medical care and is unable to travel alone.

- Transportation expenses for regular visits to see a mentally ill dependent, if these visits are recommended as a part of treatment.

Trips. Transportation to another city if the trip is primarily for, and essential to, receiving medical services are eligible. See lodging and medical conferences.

Tuition. Under special circumstances, charges for tuition are eligible. See special education. Charges for a health plan included in a lump sum tuition fee if the charges are stated separately or can easily be obtained from the school are eligible.

Vasectomy. A surgery performed to affect sterility in men.

Veterinary fees. Care of guide dogs for the seeing-impaired or hearing-impaired and other service animals specially trained to assist persons with physical disabilities are eligible.

Vision correction surgery. See eye surgery.

Weight-loss program. Amounts paid to lose weight if it is a treatment for a specific disease diagnosed by a physician, such as obesity, hypertension, or heart disease, are eligible, including fees paid for membership in a weight-reduction group and attendance at periodic meetings.

The cost of special food is eligible only if:

- The food doesn't satisfy normal nutritional needs.
- The food alleviates or treats an illness.
- The need for the food is substantiated by a physician.
- The amount included as medical expenses is limited to the amount by which the cost of the special food exceeds the cost of a normal diet.

Wheelchair. Amounts paid to rent, purchase, operate and maintain an autoette or wheelchair used mainly for the relief of sickness or disability and not just to provide transportation to and from work.

Wig. Cost of a wig purchased on the advice of a physician for the mental health of a patient who's lost all of his or her hair from disease or treatment.

X-ray. For medical reasons.

Ineligible medical and dental expenses

The following is a list of items that can't be used when figuring the medical expense deduction. The items are listed in alphabetical order.

Babysitting, childcare and nursing services for a normal healthy baby. Amounts paid for the care of children, even if the expenses enable an individual, a spouse or a dependent to get medical or dental treatment are ineligible. Any expense allowed as a childcare credit can't be treated as an expense paid for medical care.

Controlled substances. Such as marijuana, laetrile, etc., in violation of federal law.

Cosmetic surgery. Including any procedure directed at improving the patient's appearance that doesn't meaningfully promote the proper function of the body or prevent or treat illness or disease, such as face lifts, hair transplants, hair removal (electrolysis), teeth whitening and liposuction.

Dancing lessons. As well as swimming lessons, etc., even if they're recommended by a doctor, if only for the improvement of general health.

Diaper service. Diapers or diaper services, unless needed to relieve the effects of a particular disease.

Electrolysis or hair removal. See cosmetic surgery.

Employer-sponsored health insurance plan. Any insurance premiums paid by an employer-sponsored health insurance plan unless the premiums are included in box 1 of Form W-2; any other medical and dental expenses paid by the plan unless the amount paid is included in box 1 of Form W-2.

Example

Premiums paid with pre-tax dollars

You are a federal employee participating in the Federal Employee Health Benefits (FEHB) program.

Your share of the FEHB premium is paid with pretax dollars. Because you're an employee whose insurance premiums are paid with money that's never included in your gross income, you can't deduct the premiums paid with that money.

Funeral expenses. Funeral expenses may be deductible on the decedent's federal estate tax return.

Future medical care. Care to be provided substantially beyond the end of the year is ineligible. This doesn't apply to situations where the future care is purchased in connection with obtaining lifetime care of the type described under long-term care.

Hair transplant. See cosmetic surgery.

Health club dues. Or amounts paid to improve one's general health or to relieve physical or mental discomfort not related to a particular medical condition; the cost of membership in any club organized for business, pleasure, recreation or other social purpose.

Health coverage tax credit.

Household help. Even if such help is recommended by a doctor, this is a personal expense that isn't deductible. However, certain expenses paid to a person providing nursing-type services may be eligible. For more information, see nursing services. Also, certain maintenance or personal care services provided for qualified long-term care is eligible. For more information, see qualified long-term care services.

Illegal operations and treatments. Or controlled substances whether rendered or prescribed by licensed or unlicensed practitioners.

Insurance premiums. Including:

- Life insurance policies

- Policies providing payment for loss of earnings

- Policies for loss of life, limb, sight, etc.

- Policies that pay a guaranteed amount each week for a stated number of weeks if hospitalized for sickness or injury

- The part of car insurance premiums that provides medical insurance coverage for all persons injured in or by a car because the part of the premium for an individual, a spouse or a dependent isn't stated separately from the part of the premium for medical care for others

- Medicare Medigap premiums

Legal fees. Management of a guardianship estate, fees for conducting the affairs of the person being treated or other fees that aren't necessary for medical care.

Maternity clothes.

Medical savings account (MSA). Or medical expenses paid for with a tax-free distribution from an Archer MSA or other funds equal to the amount of the distribution. For more information on Archer MSAs (see IRS Publication 969—Medical Savings Accounts (MSAs)).

Nutritional supplements. Vitamins, herbal supplements, natural medicines, etc., unless recommended by a medical practitioner as treatment for a specific medical condition diagnosed by a physician.

Over-the-counter medications (except insulin). And biologicals, unless prescribed by a provider to treat a specific medical condition.

Personal-use items. The cost of an item ordinarily used for personal, living, or family purposes, unless used primarily to prevent or alleviate a physical or mental defect or illness.

For example, the cost of a toothbrush and toothpaste is a nondeductible personal expense.

An item purchased in a special form primarily to alleviate a physical defect is one that in normal form is ordinarily used for personal, living, or family purposes, the excess of the cost of the special form over the cost of the normal form is a medical expense. See braille books and magazines.

Sick leave (unused sick leave used to pay premiums).
An individual can include in gross income cash payments received at the time of retirement for unused sick leave. An individual can also include in gross income the value of unused sick leave that, at the individual's option, the employer applies to the cost of continuing participation in the employer's health plan after the individual retires. The cost of continuing participation in the health plan is eligible.

If an individual participates in a health plan where the employer automatically applies the value of unused sick leave to the cost of continuing participation in the health plan (and the individual doesn't have the option to receive cash), the individual can't include the value of the unused sick leave in gross income. The individual can't include this cost of continuing participation in that health plan as a medical expense.

Swimming lessons. See dancing lessons.

Teeth whitening. See cosmetic surgery.

Transportation expenses. Including:

- Going to and from work, even if the condition requires an unusual means of transportation
- Travel for purely personal reasons to another city for an operation or other medical care
- Travel that is merely for the general improvement of health

Weight-loss program. When for the improvement of appearance, general health or sense of well-being, including amounts paid to lose weight unless the weight loss is a treatment for a specific disease diagnosed by a physician (such as obesity, hypertension or heart disease). Includes fees paid for membership in a weight-reduction group and attendance at periodic meetings. Also membership dues for a gym, health club or spa; the cost of diet food or beverages because the diet food and beverages substitute for what is normally consumed to satisfy nutritional needs; the cost of special food unless all three of the following requirements are met:

- The food does not satisfy normal nutritional needs.
- The food alleviates or treats an illness.
- The need for the food is substantiated by a physician.

The eligible amount is limited to the amount by which the cost of the special food exceeds the cost of a normal diet.

INDEX

401(k) . . . . ii, 4, 7, 11, 83, 84, 122
529 education account, 403(b) 7

A

Above-the-line deduction 42, 104, 138, 139, 175
Account earnings 36
Account management 36, 134
Adjusted gross income 52, 104, 107, 138, 141, 175, 180
Adopted children 66, 97, 102
Adoption of plan . . . . iii, 146, 147, 148, 149, 150
Annual deductible 3, 15, 16, 17, 20, 31, 98, 120, 152
Annual limit 29, 162, 165
Archer MSA 56, 69, 118, 141, 142, 188, 208
Authorization 73, 74, 98, 100, 185

B

Bankruptcy
    Employer 43, 111
    Law 155
    Personal 36, 113, 155
Beneficiary 39, 43, 69, 114, 115, 116, 142, 158, 182
Broker 33, 38, 159

C

Cafeteria plan 9, 10, 119, 122, 138, 140, 141, 152, 153, 175, 178
Carry-over deductible 19, 21, 22
Case study 88, 90, 94
Cashless 78
Catch-up contribution 10, 44, 45, 46, 48, 52, 58, 59, 60, 104, 172
CDHP 117
Changes in employment 97
Charges 35, 36, 73, 74, 75, 99, 125, 127, 132, 187, 204
    Disputing 132
Check 36, 77, 133, 136, 153
Checkbook 39, 77, 126, 133, 135
Childcare expense 196
Child/children 9, 12, 17, 22, 23, 24, 28, 55, 60, 61, 66, 68, 85, 87, 94,
97, 102, 103, 104, 106, 110, 116, 137, 161, 177, 181, 196, 197, 201, 202, 203, 204, 206
Chronic condition 12, 88, 144, 161, 176, 198, 199
Coinsurance . . . 3, 5, 12, 15, 27, 28, 55, 74, 76, 78, 82, 85, 95, 120, 121, 131, 176, 183, 185

Index | 211

Comparability 140, 152, 153, 156
Consolidated Omnibus Budget
  Reconciliation Act (COBRA) 5, 13, 53, 70, 71, 108, 109, 110, 111, 112, 114,
                                                                                                                    115, 176, 194
Consumer Identity Program (CIP) 69
Consumer Price Index (CPI) 19
Continuous coverage 109
Contribution . . 3, 4, 7, 9, 10, 11, 16, 18, 35, 41-52, 54, 56-63, 69, 70, 80, 82, 83, 84, 85,
              88, 89, 91, 92, 93, 95, 96, 102-108, 110, 112, 114-116, 119-124, 126,
              127, 128, 130, 137-142, 146, 147, 149, 150, 152, 153, 155, 162, 163,
              166-169, 171, 172, 175, 176, 178, 180, 181, 186, 187
  Catch-up 10, 44, 45, 46, 48, 52, 58-60, 104, 172
  Excess. 3, 62, 63, 105, 106, 107, 142, 178
  Limits 3, 44, 58, 104, 166-168
  Matching. 84, 122, 140, 152, 181
  Limits for spouses 45, 58
  Maximum 3, 44, 47, 52, 57, 61, 79, 80, 103, 106, 107, 166, 168, 172, 180, 187
Co-payment . 3, 5, 15, 27, 28, 67, 74, 76, 78, 82, 87, 117, 118, 144, 176, 179, 183, 185
Coverage. . . 2, 5, 8-13, 15-22, 24, 28, 29, 31, 46, 48, 49, 51, 53, 54, 58-61, 67, 68, 71,
              85, 86, 94, 97, 102-111, 113-116, 119, 121, 124, 134, 139, 140, 142, 144,
              152, 153, 157, 160-163, 176-182, 184-187, 194, 195, 198, 207, 208
  Family . . . 9, 16, 17, 20, 21, 28, 31, 48, 51, 58-61, 68, 85, 94, 103-107, 110, 152, 153
  First-dollar. 19, 22, 24, 29, 67, 102, 160, 184
  Self-only 16, 20, 28, 48, 59, 60, 61, 103, 105-107, 110, 152, 153
Coverdell account 7
Custodial agreement. 38
Custodian . . . . ii, iv, 2, 4, 34-37, 42, 56, 72, 114, 126, 132, 135, 136, 141, 142, 148,
                                                                                                                    155, 158, 177

D

Deadline 49, 54, 63, 82, 153, 158
Death 50, 97, 101, 115, 116, 167, 177, 181, 196, 198
Debit card 35, 39, 77, 126, 133, 135
Deductible . . . 1, 2, 3, 5, 6, 12, 15, 16, 17, 19, 20-22, 26, 29, 30, 31, 42, 44, 53, 55, 61,
              73-77, 82, 83, 85-92, 94, 95, 98, 103, 109, 111, 117, 118, 120-122, 126,
              127, 128, 131, 132, 136, 138, 140, 148-153, 159, 161, 163, 166, 167, 171,
              176-180, 183-185, 187, 189, 199, 207
  Above-the-line. 42, 138, 139, 175
  Annual. 16, 17, 20, 31, 98, 120, 152
  Carry-over. 19, 21, 22
  Embedded 17, 20, 21, 85

Family 3, 17, 19, 21, 44, 61, 85
Tax 42, 83, 118, 138, 140, 163, 166, 167, 189
Deduction . . . 42, 49, 55, 61, 84, 104, 120, 123, 125, 133, 137-141, 144, 166, 169, 175
189, 193, 206
  Itemized medical 104, 133
  Payroll. 49, 55, 84, 104, 120, 166
Dental 3, 30, 31, 76, 83, 86, 117-120, 124, 163, 179, 189, 193, 206
Dental and vision 76, 83, 86, 117-120, 163
Department of Labor 108, 113, 154
Dependent. 5, 7, 8, 17, 18, 65-68, 97, 102, 103, 113, 117, 118, 137, 141, 177, 179,
181, 184, 185, 193-196, 199-204, 206, 208
Disability 5, 11, 30, 31, 50, 97, 101, 113-116, 177, 192, 196, 205
  Benefits 11, 114
Disabled 10, 114, 167, 182, 190-193, 195
Discount 13, 25, 30, 31, 39, 73, 74, 77, 99, 100, 127, 184, 185, 186
Disputing charges 132
Distribution . . 8, 11, 12, 19, 34, 36, 42, 45, 62, 65, 66, 68, 69, 72, 79, 97, 114, 123, 126,
133, 135, 141, 142, 166-168, 170, 177, 183, 186, 188, 208
  Mistaken 79, 183
Divorce 66, 97, 105-108, 116, 142, 171
Documentation 135
DOL field assistance bulletin 2004-1 154
Double-dipping 138
Dual option 149

E

Earnings . . 4, 34, 36, 61, 63, 80, 105, 118, 126, 127, 139, 167, 169, 170, 173, 178, 208
Eligibility . 8, 9, 10, 18, 29, 30, 47, 50, 54, 60, 63, 83, 97, 103, 106, 108, 109, 111, 112,
121, 124, 137, 156, 181, 184
  Eligible individual 8, 9, 11, 16-19, 41, 48, 50, 51, 57, 58, 104, 121, 138, 139, 152,
157, 177, 187
  Embedded deductible 17, 20, 21, 85
  Emergency 37, 94, 95, 97, 98, 101, 144, 161, 177, 185
Employee assistance plan (EAP) 119, 177
Employer ii, 2, 4, 5, 7, 9, 10, 12, 16-19, 26, 31, 33, 34, 35, 37, 38, 41-44, 52, 54, 58-62
71, 79, 82, 84, 87-96, 102, 103, 105, 108-115, 117-123, 126, 127, 129, 130,
133, 134, 135, 137, 139-156, 161-163, 166-169, 172, 176-179, 181, 184-186
194, 201, 206, 209
  Employer plans 154, 156
  Employer-sponsored health plan 9, 11
  Employment 42, 43, 61, 97, 116, 153, 154, 175, 181, 201

Enroll 15, 18, 38, 45, 46, 69, 102, 110, 112, 119, 148, 159, 180, 185, 195
Enrollment 10, 18, 26, 38, 46, 83, 88, 102, 110, 116, 149, 150, 160, 179, 183, 184
EOB. 126-128, 131, 135, 136
ERISA 113, 154-156, 159, 178
   Requirement 154
Excess contribution 3, 48, 62, 63, 105-107, 142, 178
Exchange 160, 161, 178, 183, 185
Excise tax 62, 63, 105, 107, 114, 152, 153, 163
Expense . 2-9, 11-13, 16, 18-22, 25-28, 30, 31, 36, 42, 45, 46, 55, 60, 61, 65-71, 76, 77
       80, 82-86, 88-90, 94-96, 99, 100, 103, 108, 109, 111-121, 123, 126, 127, 130,
          133-136, 138, 139, 141, 148, 153, 158, 170, 171, 177-179, 183-185, 187
                                        189-197, 199, 201-209
   Medical . 2, 4, 5, 7, 8, 11, 12, 16, 19, 20, 21, 27, 31, 36, 42, 45, 60, 65-70, 80, 82, 84,
         85, 89, 90, 94, 103, 108, 109, 111, 112, 114-116, 118, 120, 121, 123, 126,
         127, 133, 138, 139, 141, 158, 170, 171, 177, 179, 183, 184, 185, 189-193,
                            195-197, 199, 201, 202, 204-206, 208, 209
   Vision 76, 83, 117-120
Extension 54, 135, 158

F

Family coverage 16, 17, 20, 21, 28, 48, 58-61, 85, 94, 102-105, 107-110, 153
Family deductible 17, 21, 44
FDIC-insured 36
Federal bankruptcy law 113
Federal criteria 159
Federal HSA law 157
Federal income tax . . . . iv, 5, 159, 185
Federal Insurance Contributions Act 139, 169
Federal Unemployment Tax Act 139, 169
Fee . . 23, 26, 34-36, 75, 78, 80, 100, 127, 153, 163, 173, 180, 184, 193, 194, 196, 202,
                                                    204, 205, 208, 210
FICA 4, 7, 84, 139, 169
Fiduciary 156, 158
Financial problem 113
Form 1040 . . . . 42, 141, 142, 175, 188, 199
Form 1065 139
Form 1099-SA 42, 141, 188
Form 5329 . . . . 63, 142, 188
Form 5498-SA 42, 142, 188
Form 8889 . . . . 50, 51, 142

Form W-2 . . . . 42, 141, 153, 188, 206
Foster child 66
FSA 31, 79, 82-84, 117-124, 126, 163, 167, 175, 178, 181, 189
   Grace period 123, 124
   Limited purpose FSA (LPFSA) 83, 117, 119, 120, 124, 126
FUTA 139, 169, 201

G

Gap 5, 11, 30, 82, 86, 121, 162, 182
   Coverage 86
   Plan 30
Gatekeeper physician 73, 186
Governmental employer plans 156
Grace period 118, 119, 123, 124, 178
Grandchild 66
Great-grandchild 66
Gross income . . 45, 51, 52, 62, 66, 67, 69, 104, 106, 107, 114, 116, 137-139, 141, 175,
                                                                                                                                                                                        180, 207, 209

H

Healthcare reform 9, 24, 29, 68, 103, 146, 157, 160, 179, 183
Health insurance exchanges 160
Health insurance portability and accountability act (HIPAA) 102, 176, 179, 184
Health plan . . . ii, 1-6, 8-13, 15, 16, 22, 23, 25, 26, 28, 37-39, 41, 43, 45, 53, 68, 72-78,
               81, 83, 86, 88, 95, 98-102, 106, 109, 111, 117, 118, 124, 127, 132, 135,
               139, 145, 148, 151, 153, 154, 159, 160, 162, 163, 171, 176, 178, 179,
                                                                                    181, 183-186, 204, 209
Health reimbursement arrangement (HRA) 10, 31, 82, 84, 117-121, 123, 163,
                                                                                                                      167, 179, 189
HSA . . . .
   Administrator . . . 2, 34, 38, 39, 77, 79, 80, 86, 98, 126, 127, 132, 133, 136, 151, 183
   Custodian . . . . ii, 34, 36, 37, 132, 135, 141
   Law . . . . ii, iii, 29, 75, 86, 157
   Provider 34, 37, 38, 78, 135, 151, 170, 173
   Statement 127, 129, 132
   Trustee 34, 42, 72, 79, 114, 136, 142, 158

I

Income tax 5, 8, 11, 42, 52, 54, 57, 61, 62, 63, 66, 69, 84, 104, 105, 113-116, 126, 133, 135, 138, 139, 141, 142, 159, 166, 167, 169, 170, 173, 175, 188
  Return.......................... 5, 54, 61, 62, 116, 135, 139, 141, 142, 175, 188
Indemnity plan 30, 31, 86, 180
Individual retirement accounts 7, 34
In-network 15, 16, 20, 23, 25, 26, 28, 76, 77, 80, 83, 85, 99-101, 131, 132, 136, 161, 176, 180
  Care.. 28, 76, 77, 83, 131
  Provider 23, 26, 80, 99, 101, 131, 132, 136, 180
Insurance broker... 38
Internal revenue code 68, 155, 175, 186
Investment ... 4, 7, 19, 34, 36, 37, 80, 83, 116, 127, 129, 153, 155, 158, 166, 170, 171, 173, 177, 187
Invoices 127
IRA 7, 34, 45, 56, 57, 80, 83, 142, 166-168, 170, 172, 175, 177, 180, 188
  Roth 7, 57, 83, 167
  SEP.. 57, 168
  Transfers... 57
IRC . 4, 5, 7-11, 13, 16, 18, 24, 30, 31, 43, 45, 53, 54, 56-58, 60, 62, 63, 66-71, 86, 104, 105, 114-116, 122, 123, 135, 140, 152, 153, 155, 157, 158, 161, 163
  Section 152.. 68
  Section 213(d) 5, 121, 185
  Section 223.. 31, 157
IRS . 4-10, 13, 15, 16-21, 23, 24, 26-31, 34, 38, 41-46, 49-51, 53, 54, 56-58, 60, 61, 63, 66-72, 79, 80, 83, 84, 103, 104, 109, 113-115, 118-120, 122, 123, 125, 126, 133-136, 138-142, 152-154, 158, 159, 161, 167, 168, 177, 178, 180, 188, 189, 193, 201, 208
IRS-qualified dependents 7
Itemized medical deductions.. 133

L

Last-month rule 48, 51, 178, 180, 187
Life event 97, 102, 116, 142, 181
Lifetime limit... 29, 181
LLCs... 4, 62
Local income tax laws.. 159
Long-term care.......................... 5, 31, 70, 72, 112, 179, 194, 197-201, 207

Disability 11, 114
Expenses. 70
Insurance 31, 70, 72, 112

M

Managed care plan 73, 181, 184, 186
Marriage 61, 68, 97, 116, 181
Maximum contribution 47, 52, 79, 80, 103, 106, 168, 172, 180, 187
Medical deductions 133
Medical procedure 74, 97, 98
Medicare 4, 5, 7, 8, 10, 11, 18, 31, 45, 46, 58, 60, 71, 104, 112, 113, 115, 116, 141, 142
157, 169, 182, 185, 188, 195, 199-201, 208
Medicare Prescription Drug Improvement and Modernization Act of 2003. 157
Medigap 5, 71, 113, 182, 208
Monthly premium. 15, 82, 92, 195
MSA 56, 69, 117, 118, 141, 142, 186, 188, 208

N

Network . . 5, 13, 15, 16, 20, 23, 25, 26, 28, 39, 72-78, 80, 82, 83, 85, 98-101, 126, 131,
132, 136, 149-151, 160, 161, 175, 176, 180, 183, 185, 187
Plan 25, 26, 39, 183
Newborn. 97, 102, 161
Non-emergency 97, 98
Non-ERISA HSAs 155
Non-network care 26
Notice requirement 152

O

Office of personnel management 156, 183
Open enrollment. 26, 38, 83, 88, 102, 110, 149, 183
Out-of-network 13, 16, 20, 23, 26, 28, 75-78, 83, 99-101, 131, 132, 136, 175,
183, 187
Care. 28, 75-77, 83, 99, 131, 136
Provider 23, 26, 76, 100, 131, 136, 175, 183, 187
Out-of-pocket 3, 18, 19, 82, 84, 99, 146, 162, 177
Costs. 71, 83, 113, 182
Expense. 16, 19, 26-28, 73-75, 99, 100, 126, 131, 183
Limit 16, 19, 26-28, 73-75, 99, 100, 126, 131, 183
Maximum 3, 27, 28, 55, 82, 83, 90-92, 94, 95, 121, 149, 161

Index | 217

P

Partnership 62, 139
Patient Protection and Affordable Care Act (PPACA) 9, 157, 175, 179, 183
Patriot Act 38, 69
Payroll deduction 49, 55, 84, 120, 166, 169
Penalty 8, 53, 57, 63, 69, 74, 79, 106, 107, 113, 114, 133, 144, 160, 161, 166, 167, 170, 180, 183
Perceived risk 148
Permitted coverage 8, 29, 31, 119, 184
Personal bankruptcy 36, 155
Plan year 19, 21, 27, 54, 77, 85, 106, 118, 119, 123, 124, 151, 175, 176, 178, 183, 184
PPACA 6, 9, 11, 18, 22, 29, 68, 77, 103, 157, 159, 160, 162, 163, 175-177, 179, 181, 182, 183, 184, 185, 186
PPO 2, 25, 31, 55, 60, 89-96, 176, 180, 183, 184
Pre-existing condition 109, 160, 176, 179, 184
Premium . .2, 5, 9, 12, 13, 15, 27, 53, 60, 70, 71, 72, 82, 88, 89, 91-93, 95, 96, 109-112, 115, 143-149, 151, 161-163, 176, 179, 182-187, 194, 195, 197-199, 206-209
  Monthly 15, 82, 92, 195
Prescription 5, 27, 29, 30, 31, 80, 86, 87, 89, 90, 92, 93, 95, 118, 120, 127, 157, 161, 176, 179, 182, 203
Pre-tax 7, 11, 42, 84, 96, 117, 118, 141, 159, 168, 169, 178, 186, 207
Preventive care 6, 12, 18, 19, 22-24, 29-31, 77, 88, 121, 159, 160
Private employer plans 154
Prohibited transaction 114, 185
Prorated amount 46, 47, 52
Provider 13, 16, 20, 23, 25, 26, 33-35, 37-39, 72-80, 83, 86, 89, 91, 93, 95, 96, 99-101, 126-128, 130-132, 135, 136, 151, 170, 173, 175, 180, 181, 183-187, 200, 208
Publication 502 .... 5, 70, 189
Publication 524 115
Publication 969 .... 72, 208
Public Law No: 108-173 157

Q

Qualified healthcare expenses 3
Qualified high-deductible health plan 1, 15, 171

Qualified medical expense. . . iv, 2, 4, 5, 7, 8, 11, 31, 42, 45, 60, 65-67, 69, 70, 103, 108, 109, 112, 115, 116, 118, 123, 126, 141, 158, 170, 187, 189

R

Railroad Retirement Tax Act 139
Receipt 37, 120, 126, 127, 133, 135, 136
Record keeping. 125
Referral 73, 74, 100, 122, 177, 178, 186
Reform 9, 24, 29, 68, 103, 127, 143, 146, 157, 160, 179, 183
Refusal of charges 75
Reimbursement 10, 73, 77, 79, 82, 117, 118, 120, 121, 126, 130, 136, 178, 179, 181, 187, 200
   Duplicate. 79
Replacement plan
   Full replacement 146, 147, 149
   Gradual migration. 146
Reporting 135, 153, 156, 188
Repricing 25, 39, 77, 186
Required reporting 153
Restrictions. 72, 155
Retail price 78
Retired 10
Retiree 11, 71, 112, 113, 176
Retirement 4-8, 10, 11, 52, 121, 125, 140, 152, 165-168, 170, 172-174, 180, 186, 196, 209
Risk. 36, 41, 80, 82, 86, 98, 148, 149, 150, 163, 173
Rollover 7, 36, 56, 57, 110, 118, 119, 178, 186
   Contribution 56, 186
Roth IRA. 7, 57, 83, 167
Rules for employers 152
Run-out
   Deadline 82
   Period 119, 123

S

S Corporations 42, 139
Safe harbor. 154, 155, 186
Screening services 23, 24, 186
Self-employed. 10, 42, 59, 62, 118, 139, 175
Self-insured plan. 159, 186

Self-only coverage 16, 20, 59, 60, 103, 110
SEP IRAs 57, 168
Shoebox effect 135
Social Security Disability Insurance (SSDI) 115
Sole proprietor 61, 62
Specialist 73, 74, 99, 136, 186, 200
State estate law. 159
State insurance laws 159
State law. 68, 69, 71, 154, 155, 158, 159, 177
State mandates. 159
Statements 35, 127, 132, 135, 136, 142, 153
Stepchild. 66, 102, 116
Student. 66, 192
Submitting expenses 126
Summary plan description (SPD) 133
Suspended HRA 121

T

Tax-deductible. 42, 83, 118, 138, 140, 163, 166, 167, 189
Tax deductions 7, 137, 138, 140, 189
Tax forms 34, 141, 142
Taxpayers 5, 48, 54, 66, 69, 104, 135, 138, 175, 180, 185
Tax return . . 5, 8, 9, 18, 51, 52, 54, 61-63, 65, 66, 68, 69, 105, 107, 116, 125, 135, 137,
                                 138, 139, 141, 142, 158, 177, 185, 188, 195, 207
Testing period. 48, 50-53, 57, 63, 102, 106, 178, 180, 187
Traditional health plan. 2, 12, 15, 124
Traditional plan 2, 12, 60, 67, 76-78, 87, 103, 124, 131, 133, 148
Trend. 144, 146-148, 163, 187
Trust agreement 38, 158
Trustee 2, 34, 36, 37, 42, 56, 57, 72, 79, 110, 114, 126, 135, 136, 141, 142,
                                                                        155, 158, 187
Trustee-to-trustee transfers 36, 56, 110

U

UCR (usual, customary and reasonable) 75, 187
Umbrella deductible 21, 187
Unemployment compensation 71, 111, 112

V

Vision 3, 23, 30, 31, 58, 76, 83, 86, 117-120, 124, 161, 163, 179, 193, 194, 204

W
W-2. . . . . 42, 141, 153, 188, 206
Waiting period 36, 110, 187
Wellness program. 31, 122, 144
Withholding 139

Y
Yearly contribution limit 44
Yearly family maximum. 9
Yearly limit 7, 57

About the author

Stephen Neeleman, M.D.

Stephen Neeleman, MD is the founder and Vice Chairman of HealthEquity, Inc. (HealthEquity.com), the nation's oldest and largest dedicated health savings account custodian based in Draper, Utah. Dr. Neeleman founded HealthEquity to help people better save and spend their healthcare dollars.

As a board-certified general surgeon, Dr. Neeleman brings to HealthEquity a passion and firsthand knowledge for the practice of medicine. Prior to his medical training, Dr. Neeleman worked as general manager for Morris Air in Salt Lake City, Utah (later acquired by Southwest Airlines). Morris Air combined efficiency, technology and excellent customer service to succeed in a rocky industry. This innovative business model allowed Morris Air to rise above financially struggling competitors. With HealthEquity, Dr. Neeleman uses this model to help save another struggling industry: American healthcare.

Dr. Neeleman worked for several years as a general and trauma surgeon for Intermountain Healthcare in Utah. He currently serves as Vice Chairman, Founder, and Director for HealthEquity. Dr. Neeleman was appointed by Utah Governor Gary Herbert to serve as a board member for Utah's high-risk insurance pool and on Utah's Health Data Committee. He also serves on America's Health Insurance Plans' HSA Leadership Council and the American Bankers' Association HSA Council. Dr. Neeleman is a former assistant professor of surgery at the University of Arizona. In 2003, Dr. Neeleman spent time in Washington DC, meeting with legislators to educate them on the benefits of passing the law enabling HSAs.

Dr. Neeleman completed his undergraduate degree and played football at Utah State University. He attended medical school at the University of Utah and completed his surgical training at the University of Arizona. Dr. Neeleman is married to Christine Lamb Neeleman. Together, they have five children. They love spending time at their family's ranch in Southern Utah.

Key contributors

Sophie M. Korczyk, Ph.D.

Sophie M. Korczyk, PhD was an economist and consultant with a national consulting practice specializing in research and analysis on employee compensation and benefits with special attention to pensions, healthcare, and government budget policies in the US and overseas. Some of her clients included AARP, the World Bank, the International Monetary Fund and a number of nonprofit associations dealing with employee benefits and insurance issues. She published extensively and was a frequent speaker on compensation, benefits, and insurance issues, as well as on Social Security reform. She testified on these issues before the US Congress and several state legislatures and served as a consultant and expert witness in court cases dealing with employee benefits and compensation. She discussed managed healthcare issues on The Montel Williams Show, PBS and a number of radio stations. She was an elected member of the National Academy on Social Insurance, a nonprofit, nonpartisan organization made up of the nation's leading experts on social insurance; a Fellow of the Employee Benefit Research Institute; and a former officer of the Washington, DC. based National Economists Club. Sophie passed away in November 2009. Her contributions to help educate people through her writing remain part of her legacy.

Hazel A. Witte, J.D.

Hazel A. Witte, JD is an attorney and consultant specializing in health science, pension and benefit issues in the US and overseas. Her clients have included The US Department of Labor, The US Department of Health and Human Services, and the US Small Business Administration, the International Monetary Fund, healthcare companies, universities, and nonprofit organizations. Ms. Witte actively contributed to health-related judicial education conducted by the Einstein Institute for Science, Health and the Courts for federal and state courts and international judicial forums. She was a consultant for national programs, ASTAR–The Advanced Science and Technology Adjudication Resource Project in Washington, DC. Ms. Witte has published numerous books and articles and is a member of the District of Columbia Bar.

Joint projects

Sophie Korczyk and Hazel Witte have extensive experience as consumer educators and authors, particularly on health issues. They are co-authors of The Complete Idiot's Guide to Managed Healthcare, (New York: Alpha Books, 1998). Recommended by The Washington Post as "… well worth a day's read-through…" for its consumer-friendly information, the book is included in many consumer health education lists. Their publication HIV/AIDS and Health Insurance was featured in the Centers for Disease Control "Business Responds to AIDS" campaign. Their 2000 Executive Compensation Deskbook (San Diego, CA: Harcourt Brace Professional Publishing, 2000) is a comprehensive source of information on data and analysis dealing with executive compensation. In "Managed Care Plans in Rural Areas" (Washington, DC: National Rural Electric Cooperative Association, 1991), they compiled a series of case studies detailing the challenges and opportunities health plans face in rural communities.